The Rise of Chinese as a Global Language

Jeffrey Gil

The Rise of Chinese as a Global Language

Prospects and Obstacles

Jeffrey Gil
College of Humanities, Arts & Social Sciences
Flinders University
Adelaide, Australia

ISBN 978-3-030-76170-7   ISBN 978-3-030-76171-4   (eBook)
https://doi.org/10.1007/978-3-030-76171-4

This Palgrave Pivot imprint is published by the registered company Springer Nature
Switzerland AG
The registered company address is: Gewerbestrasse 11, 6330 Cham, Switzerland

ACKNOWLEDGEMENTS

I would like to thank the participants in this study for their time and cooperation. Part of the research for this book was conducted in China, where I visited several institutions and spoke to numerous people. I will not name these institutions or people to maintain their anonymity, but I am grateful to all of them.

I would also like to thank the editorial staff at Palgrave Macmillan for commissioning this book and guiding me through the publication process.

Some parts of this book draw on my previous work. Sections of Chapters 1, 3 and 7 are revised and updated from Gil, J. (2011). A comparison of the global status of English and Chinese: Towards a new global Language? *English Today*, 27 (1), 52–59 (Cambridge University Press). Sections of Gil, J. (2014) An exploratory study of why language learners opt for Chinese and its competitiveness as a world language. *Journal of the Chinese Language Teachers Association* 49 (1), 51–93 (The Chinese Language Teachers Association) appear in substantially revised and updated form in Chapters 1, 2, 3 and 8. A section of Chapter 5 and all of Chapter 6 were originally published as Gil, J. (2020). Will a character based writing system stop Chinese becoming a global language? A review and reconsideration of the debate. *Global Chinese*, 6 (1), 25–48 (De Gruyter). It has been revised and updated for inclusion in this book. I would like to thank the publishers for permission to reuse this material.

I first articulated the basic idea and argument of Chapter 7 in my opinion piece Gil, J. (2019, March 25). Will Mandarin be the next global language? *Asia Times* (https://www.asiatimes.com/2019/03/opinion/will-mandarin-be-the-next-global-language/). Here I present a significantly expanded and more detailed version.

Most of all, I would like to thank my family for their support and encouragement. My wife Lin Han (林函) provided much reassurance and valuable advice while I was writing this book. Our two sons, Alexander and Nicholas, asked lots of interesting questions about the book and helped choose the cover design. This book is dedicated to them.

CONTENTS

LIST OF FIGURES

LIST OF TABLES

CHAPTER 1

Introduction: Rising China, Rising Chinese

Abstract This chapter sets the macroacquisition of Chinese within the broader context of the world's language situation. It begins by describing the global language system and how macroacquisition operates within it. It then provides some essential background to the book's arguments and presents its key questions. It concludes with a brief overview of each chapter's main content and contribution to addressing the key questions.

Keywords Chinese · English as a global language · Global language system · Macroacquisition

1.1 GLOBAL "CHINESE FEVER" AS MACROACQUISITION

Since the turn of the twenty-first century, the world has been in the midst of a wave of enthusiasm for learning Chinese, often called 汉语 热 (*hànyǔ rè*) or "Chinese fever". I contend Chinese fever is connected to the reconfiguring of the world brought about by China's rise. This is because languages become important when they are associated with various forms of power, and this in turn influences their use, status and acquisition. Following on from this, I further contend that Chinese fever will have implications for the future of English as a global language.[1]

J. Gil, *The Rise of Chinese as a Global Language*, https://doi.org/10.1007/978-3-030-76171-4_1

Chinese fever involves uses of Chinese, ideas and beliefs about Chinese and decisions about Chinese, and so can be viewed as an instance of language policy broadly conceived. Spolsky (2004, 2012, 2019) defines language policy as consisting of three components: language practices, language beliefs or ideology, and language management.[2] Language practices are patterns of language use, such as what language (or variety of a language) is used for what, with whom, where and how. Language beliefs/ideology are the views, opinions and perceptions people hold towards a language (or variety of a language) and the ways in which it is used. Language management is any attempt to change or influence language practices, and maybe undertaken by a variety of actors, ranging from governments to individuals. These components are interconnected because language beliefs/ideology influence how language is used, and language practices contribute to the formation and continuation of beliefs/ideology about language. Attempts to change language practices are also based on views about how language should be used, and influence not just practices themselves but also beliefs/ideology (Liddicoat, 2013). More specifically, Chinese fever is an example of macroacquisition, or the large-scale acquisition and adoption of a language for various purposes by a range of actors (Brutt-Griffler, 2002; McKay, 2002, 2003, 2012). Before going any further, however, some background and definitions are required to set the scene for the rest of this book.

1.2   DEFINING CHINESE

Norman (1988) aptly points out that "few language names are as all-encompassing as that of Chinese" (p. 1). This name can be used to refer to the spoken and written forms of the language, all its developmental stages from earliest times to the present and all of its stylistic variations, such as literary and poetic uses (DeFrancis, 1984; Norman, 1988). Furthermore, different names are used for Chinese – Norman (1988), for example, lists seven that have been or still are used to refer to the language.

Chinese belongs to the Sinitic branch of the Sino-Tibetan family, and is very diverse with a number of varieties. The classification system used by Chinese linguists has three levels: 语言 (*yǔyán*), 方言 (*fāngyán*) and 土语 (*tǔyǔ*). *Yǔyán* means language in the sense of Chinese being a distinct language from English. *Fāngyán* is often translated as dialect, although it literally means regional speech and is used to refer to the major subdivisions within a language. *Tǔyǔ* means place language and refers to a local vernacular or form of speech (Bradley, 1992; DeFrancis, 1984). Finding English equivalents to these terms can thus cause confusion (DeFrancis, 1984; Weng, 2018). Here I follow the terminology used by Chen (1999), whereby the varieties of Chinese can be divided into dialect groups, subgroups and vernaculars and accents.

Depending on the classification system one uses, there are anywhere from seven to 13 dialect groups (Li & Zhu, 2011). These differ from each other, in some cases to the extent that they are mutually unintelligible. At the same time, all varieties of Chinese for the most part use the same written script and the differences between the varieties are largely found in phonology, with fewer in vocabulary and grammar. There is also a strong sense among the Chinese of a shared, common culture that unites speakers of all varieties as a single ethnic group (Chen, 2007; Li, 2006).

Following scholars such as Li and Zhu (2011), I therefore treat Chinese as a macrolanguage with several varieties. As shown in Table 1.1, there are generally considered to be seven dialect groups, namely Mandarin, Wu, Xiang, Yue, Kejia, Gan and Min. Each of these groups can be further divided into subgroups, which in turn can be divided into vernaculars and accents. The Mandarin group, for example, has four subgroups—Northern, Northwestern, Southwestern and Jiang-Huai— and each of these contains a number of vernaculars and accents (Chen, 1999; Norman, 1988).

Mandarin is by far the largest variety in terms of a number of speakers and geographic distribution within China, and increasingly in the Chinese diaspora. It is also the basis of national standards in China, Taiwan and Singapore[3]. I will focus primarily on Mandarin throughout this book, and in particular Modern Standard Mandarin, but I will make clear where necessary which variety (or varieties) is being discussed.

1.3   DEFINING MACROACQUISITION

According to the *Ethnologue* database, there are approximately 7,000 languages used today across the world's 200 nation states (Eberhard et al., 2020), meaning multilingualism at the individual and societal level is very common. However, languages are not acquired and used at random; we can observe patterns of multilingualism, with some languages being acquired and used by large numbers of people and others by very few. de Swaan (2001, 2013) argues these patterns of multilingualism can

Table 1.1 Classification and distribution of varieties of Chinese

Variety/dialect group	Sub-groups and distribution	Approximate percentage of speakers in China's population
Mandarin (*Běifānghuà*) 北方话	1. Northern Hebei, Henan, Shandong, Northern Anhui, Northeastern provinces, parts of Inner Mongolia 2. Northwestern Shanxi, Shaanxi, Gansu, Qinghai, Ningxia, parts of Inner Mongolia 3. Southwestern Sichuan, Yunnan, Guizhou, Northwest Guangxi, Hubei, Northwest Hunan 4. Eastern or Jiang-Huai Central Anhui, Jiangsu north of the Yangtze, Nanjing	70
Wu (*Wúyǔ*) 吴语	1. Northern Jiangsu south of the Yangtze 2. Southern Zhejiang	7.5
Xiang (*Xiāngyǔ*) 湘语	Often divided into Old Xiang and New Xiang. Spoken in Hunan	3.5
Yue (*Yuèyǔ*) 粤语	Spoken in Guangdong, Eastern Guangxi, along the southern coast (including Hong Kong and Macao) and parts of the interior	4.5
Kejia (*Kèjiāhuà*) 客家话	Spoken in parts of south China including Guangdong, Fujian, Guangxi and Jiangxi Also spoken in Taiwan	2.5
Gan (*Gànyǔ*) 赣语	Spoken in Jiangxi and southeast corner of Hubei	2

(continued)

be understood as a hierarchal structure or network, called the global language system. The global language system consists of four levels of languages: peripheral languages, central languages, supercentral languages and a hypercentral, or global, language.

Table 1.1 (continued)

Variety/dialect group	Sub-groups and distribution	Approximate percentage of speakers in China's population
Min (*Mǐnyǔ*) 闽语	1. Western Western Fujian 2. Eastern *1. Northern* Northeastern Fujian *2. Southern* Southern Fujian, parts of Guangdong and Hainan Also spoken in Taiwan	1.2 (Northern Min) 2.5 (Southern Min)

Source Compiled from data in Li (2006), Lyovin et al. (2017) and Norman (1988)

At the bottom level of the global language system are peripheral languages. While some 98% of the world's languages belong to this group, they are used by under 10% of the world's population. Peripheral languages also often lack a written script, and although they function as important vehicles of oral communication and collective memory for their native speakers, they are not often used beyond this. As such, peripheral languages have limited appeal as second or additional languages (de Swaan, 2001, 2013).

At the second level of the global language system are approximately 150 central languages. Central languages are commonly national or official languages, and are used in politics, courts, education systems, television programmes, textbooks, newspapers and the Internet. Central languages have a standard codified version and a body of classical texts associated with them. They also facilitate communication and connections between speakers of different peripheral languages. Central languages are consequently appealing as second or additional languages, as demonstrated by the fact that around 95% of the world's population uses a language belonging to this group (de Swaan, 2001, 2013).

At the third level of the global language system there are 13 supercentral languages, namely Arabic, Chinese, English, French, German, Hindi, Japanese, Malay, Portuguese, Russian, Spanish, Swahili and Turkish, some of which have over 100 million speakers. These languages facilitate communication and connections between speakers of different central languages, often across vast distances and in a wide range of domains, thus giving them great appeal as second or additional languages (de Swaan, 2001, 2013).

At the fourth and highest level of the global language system is one hypercentral, or global, language, namely English. English is the one language that "connects the supercentral languages with one another and that therefore constitutes the pivot of the world language system" (de Swaan, 2001, p. 6). English is widely perceived to bring a range of benefits, including access to knowledge, employment, education and social status, and is used in many areas of life, such as science, business and diplomacy. Consequently, English language learning is immensely popular all over the world.

Coupland (2013) says the global language system depicts "an evolving set of relationships among languages as their utility values change" (p. 9). The value of languages is heavily influenced by the broader political, economic, cultural and social contexts in which they exist, so that changes in this broader context have important implications for their use, status and acquisition as second or additional languages[4]. Within the confines of this context, people are generally drawn to the language(s) most closely associated with various kinds of resources, and perceived to bring the most benefits. It is here the concept of macroacquisition is useful.

In her original conceptualisation of macroacquisition based on the spread of English around the world, Brutt-Griffler (2002) defined it as "the spread of language to new speech communities via a process of second language acquisition" (p. 136). A speech community could be national, regional, international, ethnic or occupational, and an individual could be a member of more than one (Brutt-Griffler, 2002). Brutt-Griffler (2002) also distinguished between two kinds of macroacquisition, Type A and Type B. Type A macroacquisition occurred in multilingual contexts where there was no existing and well-established national language common to the population. In such cases, a new speech community developed in which English came to serve as a national language or intranational lingua franca, and a new variety of English also developed. This occurred in Nigeria, India and Singapore, among other countries. Type B macroacquisition, in contrast, involved a mainly monolingual speech community, or at least part of it, changing into a bilingual speech community. This type of macroacquisitionoccurred in contexts with an existing and well-established national language common to the population. Here English did not become an intranational lingua franca and no new speech community or variety developed. Countries such as Japan and Mexico exemplify this kind of macroacquisition (Brutt-Griffler, 2002). Macroacquisitionis useful for explaining the spread of English and has been taken up by other scholars (e.g. McKay, 2002, 2003, 2012; Zhou, 2006). But it is not without its shortcomings. Firstly, the notion of a speech community has been questioned on the grounds that it portrays uniformity, is based on social categories which are assumed to be fixed and does not account for the role of individuals in creating their own affiliations (Martin-Jones et al., 2012). Of particular relevance to this project is that I am not looking at one specific speech community but rather a variety of entities that are acquiring Chinese. Furthermore, the assumption that speech communities in Type B macroacquisition need to be monolingual is not warranted given the prevalence of multilingualism in the world. In many cases, those acquiring another language will not be monolingual. In place of speech communities then, I prefer to use the term actors, and view them as engaging in the language policy of adding Chinese to their linguistic repertoires through macroacquisition. As Shohamy (2006) explains, a range of actors can have language policy, from those "as small as individuals and families" to "larger entities, such as schools, cities, regions, nations, territories or in the global context" (p. 48).

Macroacquisition is also similar to the concept of investment developed by Bonny Norton across a range of publications (see for example Norton, 2000; Norton & Gao, 2008; Norton Peirce, 1995). This concept can flesh out the mechanics of macroacquisition. Investment refers to learners' commitment to the second/additional language, that is, the time, money and effort they put into its acquisition. Learners invest in a second/additional language with the expectation that it will bring them material and symbolic rewards or benefits such as money, education and knowledge. Importantly, and in line with what has been said above, the broader political, economic, cultural and social context around learners is seen to influence which language(s) they invest in (Norton, 2000; Norton Peirce, 1995; Pavlenko, 2002). In order to add Chinese to their linguistic repertoires, actors therefore invest time, money and effort, with the expectation that they will benefit from this.

Macroacquisition is prompted by both the objective association of a language with various resources and actors' subjective perceptions. The objective aspect of macroacquisition refers to the current standing of, uses and resources available in and through a language. This covers language practices and reflects language management. The subjective aspect, meanwhile, refers to ideas and beliefs about a language's association with various resources. This covers language beliefs/ideology. Several developments suggest the macroacquisitionof Chinese is well underway.

1.4   SIGNS OF THE MACROACQUISITION OF CHINESE

According to some estimates, 100 million people are now studying Chinese (*China Daily*, 2017). Just as significant as the numbers is that this interest in Chinese is found in contexts where it previously did not exist, at least not to a significant extent. In some parts of Africa, for example, where European colonial languages such as English and French have traditionally dominated second or additional language education, students are increasingly interested in learning Chinese because of job opportunities created by China's investment, ease of getting study visas following restrictions put in place by the USA and Europe, and less expensive tuition fees in Chinese universities (Einashe, 2018). Increasing numbers of bilingual Chinese/English schools are opening worldwide. Over 200 now exist in the USA, along with smaller numbers in the UK and Australia (Kelly, 2017; Nicholson, 2016).

Organisations are also endeavouring to equip their personnel with Chinese language proficiency. For example, police officers in southern Brisbane, the capital city of the state of Queensland, Australia, have been learning Chinese to facilitate communication with people in suburbs with substantial Chinese populations (Vujkovic, 2019). A similar initiative was undertaken by police in Auckland, New Zealand (Walters, 2018). In the Philippines, government employees of the Presidential Communications Operations Office (PCOO) are learning Chinese to be able to better communicate with Chinese officials (Romero, 2019).

The options for learning Chinese have similarly increased, ranging from government schools to private providers to online platforms, and there has been a proliferation of textbooks, teaching materials and other learning aids (Tsung & Cruickshank, 2011). Certification of Chinese language competence is also increasingly desirable, as demonstrated by the number of people taking the Chinese Proficiency Test (HSK) (汉语水平考试 *hànyǔ shuǐpíng kǎoshì*). In 2017 alone, some 770,000 people took the various forms of the HSK (Hanban, 2017).

Several media reports have noted wealthy and influential people seeking Chinese language education for their children. These include

Amazon founder Jeff Bezos, Facebook CEO Mark Zuckerberg, royal couple Prince William and Kate Middleton, and Ivanka Trump and Jared Kushner (Jackson, 2017). American businessman Jim Rogers also relocated his family to Singapore so his daughters could acquire Chinese. The presence of Chinese in physical and virtual space has also increased. For example, many airports around the world have installed Chinese language signage, including Sydney (Australia), Christchurch (New Zealand), Moscow (Russia), Helsinki (Finland) and Minsk (Belarus) (Airport World, 2013; BelarusFeed, 2017; Creedy, 2018; Mu, 2017; O'Meara, 2019) (Fig. 1.1).

The Victorian state government in Australia recently installed a number of road safety signs on major roads, including the famous Great Ocean Road, and the Western Australia state government installed multilingual signage, including Chinese, along major tourist routes and stretches of road known to be dangerous (Himmelreich, 2017; McCubbing, 2019; Websdane, 2019). The South Australian Tourism Commission funded

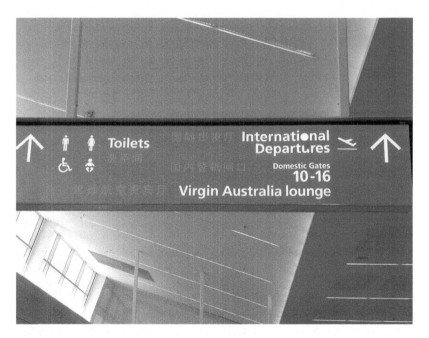

Fig. 1.1   Chinese language signage at Adelaide Airport, Australia

the smartphone app UWAI (游外 *yóu wài*, meaning "travel abroad") to assist Chinese tourists to find their way around during their stay in the state. The app allows tourists to scan a code displayed on a sign to get information in Chinese about hotels, shops and other businesses. UWAI is currently used by around 850 businesses (South Australian Tourism Commission, 2017) (Figs. 1.2 and 1.3).

A similar digital service, known as MyHelsinki, was launched by the Helsinki Tourism Office in 2019. MyHelsinki works through the Chinese social media and messaging app WeChat, and is intended to facilitate independent travel by providing Chinese language information about sightseeing and travel options. It also enables tourists to pay for public transport via WeChat Pay (O'Meara, 2019). This leads to the first question this book proposes: *What is driving the macroacquisition of Chinese?*

Chapters 2–5 address this question. I set out the conceptual framework, as well as the sources and methods which I employ to investigate the macroacquisitionof Chinese, in Chapter 2. I use a modified version of Xu's (2007) language comprehensive competitiveness (语言综合竞争力 *yǔyán zōnghé jìngzhēng lì*) framework to define and describe the resources which drive the macroacquisition of Chinese. There are eight components to this framework—policy, cultural, economic, population, script, scientific/technological, educational and geostrategic competitiveness. To discuss the objective perspective of language comprehensive competitiveness, I draw on academic works, media and Internet sources relevant to each component of language comprehensive competitiveness. For the subjective perspective, I use a survey of Chinese language students at tertiary institutions in Australia and China, email interviews with Chinese language students at tertiary institutions in Australia, interviews with Chinese language teachers at tertiary institutions in Australia and China and interviews with scholars at a research institute in China.

Chapter 3 presents the objective perspective on the language comprehensive competitiveness of Chinese. I argue geostrategic, economic and population competitiveness most strongly support the macroacquisition of Chinese in objective terms, while policy, cultural, scientific/technological and educational competitiveness offer somewhat less support. Script competitiveness provides the least support for the macroacquisition of Chinese in objective terms. Chapter 4 covers the language comprehensive competitiveness of Chinese from the subjective perspective. Here I show that geostrategic, population and economic

Fig. 1.2 A restaurant in Adelaide, Australia with UWAI

Fig. 1.3   A close up of the UWAI sign

competitiveness most strongly support the macroacquisition of Chinese
in subjective terms. Cultural, policy and educational competitiveness also
offer some support but not as much as these components, and script
competitiveness less so. Finally, scientific/technological competitiveness
offers the least support for macroacquisition. Chapter 5 combines the
findings of the previous two chapters to produce a language comprehensive competitiveness profile of Chinese. I categorise the components
of language comprehensive competitiveness into strenths (geostrategic,
economic and population competitiveness), intermediates (policy, cultural
and educational competitiveness) and weaknesses (script and scien-
tific/technological competitiveness). Chapters 6 and 7 shift focus to the
implications of the macroacquisition of Chinese for the future of English
as a global language. Once again, some background and definitions are in
order.

1.5   Defining Global Language

The earlier discussion of the global language system showed English is
in a unique position among the world's languages. No other language
has ever achieved the status of English, and it appears well-entrenched as
a global language. McArthur (2005) defines global language as "a late
20c term for a language used everywhere on earth (and usually linked
to English)" (p. 257). This definition is intuitively appealing, but needs

to be fleshed out. Ammon (2013) goes some way towards this with his concept of the "globality of languages" (p. 101). Globality denotes the condition of something existing across the world and acting as a way of facilitating interconnections between people, as well as people's awareness of this state of affairs (Axford, 2013; Scholte, 2005). According to Ammon (2013), a language's globality consists of its global status (i.e. geographical coverage), global function (i.e. its use for global communication) and the factors which influence global function (i.e. the reasons why a language is used for global communication). He also points out that languages can have different degrees of globality, and as such the globality of languages can be compared.

Yet we still need to describe how global status and global function manifest themselves. Crystal (2003) further specifies the characteristics of a global language when he says that a global language is a language that has "a special role that is recognized in every country" (p. 3). This special role consists of three components: native language, official language and foreign language. The native language component of this special role refers to the language being the first language of the majority of people in some countries. The second component refers to the status of the language as an official or co-official language in various countries. In such cases, it is the principal language of government, broadcasting, the media and the education system. Finally, the foreign language component means the language is given priority in language teaching and learning. In Crystal's (2006) words, it is "the foreign language which children are most likely to encounter when they arrive in school, and the one most available to adults in further education" (p. 423). This does not imply that everyone in the world uses English for all purposes; indeed, there are millions of people who do not speak English and places where its use is very limited, but they are nevertheless aware of English and its position in the world (McArthur, 2004).

These characteristics of a global language are reflected in Kachru's (1985, 1988, 1992, 2005) Three Circles Model. According to this model, the use and status of English can be depicted as three concentric circles, called the Inner Circle, Outer Circle and Expanding Circle. The Inner Circle comprises countries such as Britain, America, Canada, Australia and New Zealand, where English is spoken natively and is the primary language of society. The Outer Circle encompasses countries where English was introduced through colonisation from Inner Circle countries. In these countries, English has important intranational functions, such as being an official language or the medium of instruction in the education system. India, Kenya and Singapore are typical examples of Outer Circle countries. The Expanding Circle consists of countries that were not colonised by Inner Circle countries and where English is not used to any significant extent intranationally. Proficiency in English is perceived as a valuable asset for interacting with the rest of the world and is used mainly for such purposes, including international trade and tourism. English is taught as a subject in schools. Many countries fall into the Expanding Circle, including China, Japan, Vietnam and Russia, to give just a few examples. This model is used in most studies of English as a global language.

It is not without its problems, however. Firstly, it does not account well for the differences between Inner Circle varieties of English. As McArthur (1998) points out, differences exist within Inner Circle countries (for example the many regional and social dialects of Britain or the USA) and across Inner Circle countries (for example the differences between Standard Australian and Standard American English), and these may be significant enough to impede communication. This calls into question whether all such countries can be grouped together. Another issue is that there are communities of native English speakers residing in the Outer and Expanding Circles, such as the Anglo-Indian community in India, the British expatriate community in Hong Kong and the Anglo-Argentine community in Argentina. Likewise, there are communities of non-native English speakers residing in the Inner Circle, including migrants and international students (Galloway & Rose, 2015; McArthur, 1998). The use and status of English in the Expanding Circle has also changed since Kachru first proposed his model. English has growing intranational functions in many Expanding Circle countries in domains such as business, education and the media, which blurs the line between them and Outer Circle countries (Galloway & Rose, 2015).

Thirdly, the existence of English-based pidgins and creoles in all three circles also poses problems. It is unclear how these fit into the model or whether they should be seen as varieties of English or distinct languages. The model similarly does not account for hybrid uses of English, such as code mixing and code switching with other languages (Galloway & Rose, 2015; McArthur, 1998). Again, it is not always possible to definitively classify countries into the Inner, Outer or Expanding Circle.

Finally, the model suggests, albeit unintentionally, that native speakers are superior to other speakers of English. The labelling of native English speaking countries as the Inner Circle gives the impression that native speakers are the most authoritative, competent and representative speakers of English (Jenkins, 2014; McArthur, 1998). This is not necessarily the case because, as Jenkins (2014) explains, "the fact that English is somebody's second or subsequent language does not mean that their competence is, by definition, lower than that of a native speaker" (p. 16).

While the Three Circles Model can be regarded as an oversimplification, no model could hope to fully capture the increasingly complex reality of a language's global situation (McArthur, 1998, 2002). It still provides a useful foundation for conceptualising what it means for a language to be global because it covers Ammon's (2013) global status and global function. The language comprehensive competitiveness framework complements this by describing the factors which influence global function. This combination will therefore inform my discussion of the global standing of Chinese.

1.6   The Future of English as a Global Language

English became a global language because it was associated with the two most powerful and influential countries of modern times, firstly Britain, the leading colonial power during the seventeenth and eighteenth centuries, and the originator of the Industrial Revolution in the nineteenth century, then the USA, the world's leading economic, political, scientific and cultural power throughout the twentieth century and into the early twenty-first century. For some time now, scholars have predicted English will remain a global language well into the future. For example, while Wardhaugh (1987) acknowledged the possibility of another language becoming a global language, he said "such a possibility would appear in the late twentieth century to require some kind of political or natural catastrophe to bring it about" (p. 14). A decade later, Honey (1997) argued that:

"English is the world language—at least for the next five hundred years, or until the Martians arrive. Something like a quarter of the total population of the globe now speak, or are trying to learn, English—a proportion without precedent in the history of the world" (p. 249).

Not long after this, Bruthiaux (2002) argued "the worldwide dominance of English is such that only catastrophic upheaval could seemingly threaten it in the near future" (p. 129). More recently, MacKenzie (2018) asserted that "English as an international lingua franca probably has a long future ahead of it as a major component of multilingual communicators' repertoires" (p. 100).

The common theme to these statements is that dislodging English as a global language would require a truly momentous event. China's rise could justifiably be described as such an event. It will have profound effects on the world, including potentially reshaping the global language system. Indeed, history demonstrates that once the circumstances which encourage the macroacquisition of a language cease to exist, its position within the global language system will decline (see, for example, the discussions in Chew, 2009; Ostler, 2010; Wright, 2016). English may not be a global language forever if acquiring and using another language proves to be more beneficial. This leads to this book's second question: *What are the implications of the macroacquisition of Chinese for the future of English as a global language?*

Chapters 6 and 7 deal with this question. Most academics and media commentators argue a character-based writing system will prevent Chinese becoming a global language because it is difficult and time-consuming to learn. In Chapter 6 I present a counterargument. I show this view is based on flawed assumptions about proficiency, does not account for the use of technology in learning and using characters, ignores a historical precedent for the use of characters beyond China and focuses too much on linguistic properties. Whether Chinese establishes an association with the various forms of power outlined in the language comprehensive competitiveness framework sufficient to make it a global language will depend on the outcome of China's rise, and this is the subject of Chapter 7. I present three possible scenarios—continuation, in which English remains a global language; coexistence, in which English and Chinese are both global languages; and replacement, in which Chinese becomes a global language instead of English—and discuss how they connect to the possible outcomes of China's rise. Chapter 8 rounds out the book by summarising its main findings and making suggestions for further research.

Vaish (2010) argues that the use and status of Chinese on the global level has not received adequate attention from applied linguists. In this book I hope to go some way towards addressing this by providing a conceptually and empirically based analysis of the macroacquisition of Chinese and its implications for the future of English as a global language.

NOTES

1. For the sake of convenience and clarity, I use conventional names to refer to languages (English, Chinese etc.). As Ricento (2015) points out, such names have a "psychological reality" (p. 296), even though the form and function of such languages may vary considerably across geographic regions and social groups. "English" and "Chinese" might therefore refer to very different linguistic forms and functions in practice. Such issues are discussed at various points in this book.
2. Spolsky uses the term "language management" instead of "language planning".
3. This should not be taken to imply that the status of Mandarin (and particularly its standardised versions) is universally accepted or uncontested. The relationship between Mandarin and other varieties of Chinese will be discussed at various points in this book.
4. I explore the evolution of the global language system in detail in Chapter 2.

REFERENCES

Airport World. (2013). *Airport introduces Chinese signs while staff learn basic phrases*. Retrieved 5 August 2019, from http://www.airport-world.com/news/general-news/2775-airport-introduces-chinese-signs-and-staff-to-learn-basic-phrases.html

Ammon, U. (2013). World languages: Trends and futures. In N. Coupland (Ed.), *The handbook of language and globalization* (pp. 101–122). Wiley-Blackwell.

Axford, B. (2013). *Theories of globalization*. Polity Press.

BelarusFeed. (2017). *Minsk airport gets info signs in Chinese language*. Retrieved 5 August, 2019, from https://belarusfeed.com/airport-chinese-introduced/

Bradley, D. (1992). Chinese as a pluricentric language. In M. Clyne (Ed.), *Pluricentric languages: Differing norms in different nations* (pp. 305–324). Mouton de Gruyter.

Bruthiaux, P. (2002). Predicting challenges to English as a global language in the 21st century. *Language Problems & Language Planning, 26*(2), 129–157.

Brutt-Griffler, J. (2002). *World English: A study of its development*. Multilingual Matters.

Chen, P. (1999). *Modern Chinese: History and sociolinguistics*. Cambridge University Press.

Chen, P. (2007). China. In A. Simpson (Ed.), *Language and national identity in Asia* (pp. 141–167). Oxford University Press.

Chew, P. G. L. (2009). *Emergent lingua francas and world orders: The politics and place of English as a world language*. Routledge.

China Daily. (2017). *Mandarin is now rapidly becoming a global language.* Retrieved 15 February 2019, from http://www.chinadaily.com.cn/opinion/2017-10/13/content_33190150.htm

Coupland, N. (2013). Introduction: Sociolinguistics in the global era. In N. Coupland (Ed.), *The handbook of language and globalization* (pp. 56–76). Wiley-Blackwell.

Creedy, S. (2018, February 8). Sydney airport rolls out the welcome mat for Chinese growth. *The Airport Professional.* Retrieved 5 August, 2019, from https://airportprofessional.asn.au/major-airports/sydney-airport-rolls-welcome-mat-chinese-growth/

Crystal, D. (2003). *English as a global language* (2nd ed.). Cambridge University Press.

Crystal, D. (2006). English worldwide. In R. Hogg & D. Denison (Eds.), *A history of the English language* (pp. 420–439). Cambridge University Press.

DeFrancis, J. (1984). *The Chinese language: Fact and fantasy.* University of Hawaii Press.

de Swaan, A. (2001). *Words of the world: The global language system.* Polity Press.

de Swaan, A. (2013). Language systems. In N. Coupland (Ed.), *The handbook of language and globalization* (pp. 56–76). Wiley-Blackwell.

Eberhard, D. M., Simons, G. F. & Fennig, C. D. (Eds.). (2020). *Ethnologue: Languages of the world* (23rd ed.). Retrieved 19 February 2021, from http://www.ethnologue.com

Einashe, I. (2018, May 16). How Mandarin is conquering Africa via Confucius Institutes and giving China a soft-power advantage. *South China Morning Post.* Retrieved 17 May 2019, from https://www.scmp.com/lifestyle/article/2146368/how-mandarin-conquering-africa-confucius-institutes-and-giving-china-soft

Galloway, N., & Rose, H. (2015). *Introducing global Englishes.* Routledge.

Hanban. (2017). *Confucius Institute Annual Development Report 2017.* Retrieved 22 April 2019, from http://www.hanban.org/report/2017.pdf

Himmelreich, E. (2017, March 25). Chinese road signs coming for Great Ocean Road. *The Standard.* Retrieved 6 August 2019, from https://www.standard.net.au/story/4554272/chinese-signs-coming/

Honey, J. (1997). *Language is power: The story of Standard English and its enemies.* Faber and Faber.

Jackson, A. (2017, November 9). Billionaires and royals are rushing to teach their kids Mandarin. *Independent.* Retrieved 26 November 2019, from https://www.independent.co.uk/life-style/billionaires-and-royals-are-rushing-to-teach-their-kids-mandarin-a8045891.html

Jenkins, J. (2014). *Global Englishes: A resource book for students* (3rd ed.). Routledge.

Kachru, B. B. (1985). Standards, codification and sociolinguistic realism: The English language in the outer circle. In R. Quirk & H. G. Widdowson (Eds.), *English in the world: Teaching and learning the language and literatures* (pp. 11–30). Cambridge University Press.
Kachru, B. B. (1988). The sacred cows of English. *English Today, 4*(4), 3–8.
Kachru, B. B. (1992). Teaching World Englishes. In B. Kachru (Ed.), *The other tongue: English across cultures* (2nd ed., pp. 355–365). University of Illinois Press.
Kachru, B. B. (2005). *Asian Englishes: Beyond the canon.* Hong Kong University Press.
Kelly, G. (2017, June 7). Are Chinese-English bilingual schools the future of primary education? *The Telegraph.* Retrieved 8 January, 2019, from https://www.telegraph.co.uk/education/2017/06/07/chinese-english-bilingual-schools-future-primary-education/
Li, D. C. S. (2006). Chinese as a lingua franca in greater China. *Annual Review of Applied Linguistics, 26,* 149–176.
Li, W., & Zhu, H. (2011). Changing hierarchies in Chinese language education for the British learners. In L. Tsung & K. Cruickshank (Eds.), *Teaching and learning Chinese in global contexts: Multimodality and literacy in the new media age* (pp. 11–27). Continuum.
Liddicoat, A. J. (2013). *Language-in-education policies: The discursive construction of intercultural relations.* Multilingual Matters.
Lyovin, A. V., Kessler, B., & Leben, W. R. (2017). *An introduction to the languages of the world* (2nd ed.). Oxford University Press.
MacKenzie, I. (2018). *Language contact and the future of English.* Routledge.
Martin-Jones, M., Blackledge, A., & Creese, A. (2012). Introduction: A sociolinguistics of multilingualism for our times. In M. Martin-Jones, A. Blackledge, & A. Creese (Eds.), *The Routledge handbook of multilingualism* (pp. 1–26). Routledge.
McArthur, T. (1998). *The English languages.* Cambridge University Press.
McArthur, T. (2002). *The Oxford guide to world English.* Oxford University Press.
McArthur, T. (2004). Is it *world* or *international* or *global* English, and does it matter? *English Today, 20*(3), 3–15.
McArthur, T. (2005). *Concise Oxford companion to the English language.* Oxford University Press.
McCubbing, G. (2019, February 8). Homemade Chinese language signs replaced by state government. *The Standard.* Retrieved 6 August 2019, from https://www.standard.net.au/story/5892850/chinese-new-year-on-the-great-ocean-road-a-sign-of-the-times-but-illegal/
McKay, S. (2002). *Teaching English as an international language: Rethinking goals and approaches.* Oxford University Press.

McKay, S. (2003). Toward an appropriate EIL pedagogy: Re-examining common ELT assumptions. *International Journal of Applied Linguistics, 13*(1), 1–22.

McKay, S. (2012). Teaching materials for English as an international language. In A. Matsuda (Ed.), *Principles and practices of teaching English as an international language* (pp. 70–83). Multilingual Matters.

Mu, S. (2017, November 16). Chinese language use growing in Russia. *China Plus*. Retrieved 5 August 2019, from http://chinaplus.cri.cn/news/china/9/20171116/52989.html

Nicholson, M. (2016, April 20). Chinese language classes to make up 50 per cent of lessons at South Australian school. *SBS*. Retrieved 31 January 2019, from https://www.sbs.com.au/topics/life/culture/article/2016/04/19/chinese-language-classes-make-50-cent-lessons-south-australian-school

Norman, J. (1988). *Chinese*. Cambridge University Press.

Norton, B. (2000). *Identity and language learning: Gender, ethnicity and educational change*. Pearson Education Limited.

Norton, B., & Gao, Y. (2008). Identity, investment, and Chinese learners of English. *Journal of Asian Pacific Communication, 18*(1), 109–120.

Norton Peirce, B. (1995). Social identity, investment, and language learning. *TESOL Quarterly, 29*(1), 9–31.

O'Meara, S. (2019, July 24). Helsinki uses WeChat to encourage more Chinese tourists to see the real side of Finland. *South China Morning Post*. Retrieved 25 July 2019, from https://www.scmp.com/print/lifestyle/travel-leisure/article/3019609/helsinki-uses-wechat-encourage-more-chinese-tourists-see

Ostler, N. (2010). *The last lingua franca: English until the return of Babel*. Walker Publishing Company.

Pavlenko, A. (2002). Poststructuralist approaches to the study of social factors in second language learning and use. In V. Cook (Ed.), *Portraits of the L2 user* (pp. 277–302). Multilingual Matters.

Ricento, T. (2015). "English", the global lingua franca? In T. Ricento (Ed.), *Language policy and political economy: English in global context* (pp. 276–304). Oxford University Press.

Romero, A. (2019, April 15). PCOO staff learning Chinese language. *The Philippine Star*. Retrieved 23 September, 2019 from https://www.philstar.com/headlines/2019/04/15/1910126/pcoo-staff-learning-chinese-language

Scholte, J. A. (2005). *Globalization: A critical introduction* (2nd ed.). Palgrave Macmillan.

Shohamy, E. (2006). *Language policy: Hidden agendas and new approaches*. Routledge.

South Australian Tourism Commission. (2017). *Smartphone app launched for Chinese visitors*. Retrieved 5 August 2019, from https://tourism.sa.gov.au/news-and-media/news/2017/sep/08/smartphone-app-launched-for-chinese-visitors

Spolsky, B. (2004). *Language policy.* Cambridge University Press.
Spolsky, B. (2012). What is language policy? In B. Spolsky (Ed.), *The Cambridge handbook of language policy* (pp. 3–15). Cambridge University Press.
Spolsky, B. (2019). A modified and enriched theory of language policy (and management). *Language Policy, 18*(3), 323–338.
Tsung, L., & Cruickshank, K. (2011). Emerging trends and issues in teaching and learning Chinese. In L. Tsung & K. Cruickshank (Eds.), *Teaching and learning Chinese in global contexts: Multimodality and literacy in the new media age* (pp. 1–10). Continuum.
Vaish, V. (2010). Introduction: Globalization of language and culture in Asia. In V. Vaish (Ed.), *Globalization of language and culture in Asia: The impact of globalization processes on language* (pp. 1–13). Continuum.
Vujkovic, M. (2019, July 17). Queensland police learn Mandarin in bid to target crime concerns. *ABC News.* Retrieved 19 July 2019, from https://www.abc.net.au/news/2019-07-17/queensland-police-learn-chinese-launch-operation-against-crime/11303386
Walters, L. (2018, October 15). Police Chinese language classes trialled in Auckland. *Newsroom.* Retrieved 23 September 2019, from https://www.newsroom.co.nz/2018/10/14/274143/police-chinese-language-classes-trialled-in-auckland
Wardhaugh, R. (1987). *Languages in competition: Dominance, diversity, and decline.* Basil Blackwell.
Websdane, D. (2019, November 1). West Australian government installs foreign language signs on deadly tourist roads. *9 News.* Retrieved 7 November 2019, from https://www.9news.com.au/national/west-australian-government-rolls-out-foreign-language-signs-on-deadly-tourist-roads/d42701e6-b22b-4ef9-b9fa-2ab675a0d0fa
Weng, J. (2018). What is Mandarin? The social project of language standardization in early Republican China. *The Journal of Asian Studies, 77*(3), 611–633.
Wright, S. (2016). *Language policy and language planning: From nationalism to globalisation* (2nd ed.). Palgrave Macmillan.
Xu, J. (2007). 语言规划与语言教育 *Language planning and language education.* Xuelin Press.
Zhou, M. (2006). Theorizing language contact, spread, and variation in status planning: A case study of Modern Standard Chinese. *Journal of Asian Pacific Communication, 16*(2), 159–174.
Zhou, M. (2019). *Language ideology and order in rising China.* Palgrave Macmillan.

CHAPTER 2

The Macroacquisition of Chinese in the Global Ecology of Languages

Abstract This chapter sets the macroacquisition of Chinese within the global ecology of languages. It uses the punctuated equilibrium model to trace how this ecology produced the current global language system, in which central and supercentral languages, and especially the hypercentral language, English, are most associated with power and perceived to be desirable to acquire and use. It then argues China's rise is the latest in a series of events to reshape the global language system. Following this, it argues that language comprehensive competitiveness is an appropriate conceptual framework for defining and describing the various forms of power which may drive the macroacquisition of Chinese. It defines language comprehensive competitiveness and traces its development, then sets out each of its components. It also makes the case for the inclusion of additional components which need to be considered when studying the macroacquisition of a language.

Keywords China's rise · Ecology of language · Global language · Language comprehensive competitiveness · Punctuated equilibrium model

© The Author(s), under exclusive license to Springer Nature Switzerland AG 2021
J. Gil, *The Rise of Chinese as a Global Language*,
https://doi.org/10.1007/978-3-030-76171-4_2

2.1   Introduction

The ecology of language approach has been widely employed as a way to understand multilingual situations. This approach is relevant to understanding the macroacquisitionof Chinese because, as Hornberger and Hult (2008) point out, it shows how actors' acquisition and use of second/additional languages are connected to the broader state of affairs in the world. With this in mind, I use this chapter to set the macroacquisition of Chinese within the global ecology of languages. I use the punctuated equilibrium model (Dixon, 1997; Nettle & Romaine, 2000) to trace how this ecology has changed to produce the current global language system, in which central and supercentral languages, and especially the hypercentral language, English, are most associated with power and perceived to be desirable to acquire and use. I then argue China's rise is the latest in a series of events to reshape the global language system. Following this, I argue that language comprehensive competitiveness is an appropriate conceptual framework for defining and describing the various forms of power which may drive the macroacquisitionof Chinese. I define language comprehensive competitiveness and trace its development, then set out each of its components. I also make the case for the inclusion of additional components I believe need to be considered when studying the macroacquisition of a language.

With this conceptual framework in place, I then shift focus to the sources and methods I use to investigate the macroacquisition of Chinese. I explain what data I use as evidence to establish which components of language comprehensive competitiveness are responsible for the macroacquisition of Chinese and how I gathered it.

2.2   Global Ecology of Languages

Haugen (1972) proposed the notion of the ecology of language to describe the connection between languages and the broader political, economic, cultural, social and environmental contexts in which they exist. He defined it as "the study of interactions between any given language and its environment" (1972, p. 325 cited in Mühlhäusler, 2010, p. 422).[1] Ecology here is intended as a metaphor to demonstrate how languages are linked to and affected by these broader contexts (Hult, 2013). Just as changes in an ecosystem affect plants and animals, so too do political, economic, cultural, social and environmental changes have major implications for languages.

Within any particular ecology,[2] each language has its own niche, or set of domains and functions. A language may have a greater or lesser niche compared to other languages present in the ecology, and it is the above factors that determine its nature and extent, and in turn how that language is perceived (Calvet, 2006; Hornberger & Hult, 2008; Hult, 2013). Mühlhäusler (2010) and Grenoble (2011) argue that differences in power among various actors result in competitive language ecologies. In this kind of ecology, the languages of the more powerful actors spread and are accorded prestige at the expense of others. The global language system can be thought of as a competitive language ecology in which a small number of languages dominate because of the power of those who speak them.

2.3   THE PUNCTUATED EQUILIBRIUM MODEL

The punctuated equilibrium model, put forward by Dixon (1997) and later adopted by Nettle and Romaine (2000), can be employed to describe how this state of affairs was created.[3] According to this model, a language ecology can be in one of two states: equilibrium or punctuation. Equilibrium is a state of stability and relative harmony among people and languages. During periods of equilibrium, each group of people would have a roughly similar lifestyle, level of technological sophistication and access to resources. Consequently, no one group—and by extension language—would be drastically bigger, stronger or more prestigious than any of the others. Many groups and their languages would coexist on a roughly equal basis. This does not mean that there was no change at all; a language might expand as one group was incorporated into another, or a language might cease to exist as a result of its speakers dying from any number of causes. However, during periods of equilibrium such occurrences would be relatively rare and would have happened only on a small scale. There would not have been large numbers of languages disappearing or one language becoming dominant over a large area (Dixon, 1997).

Equilibrium can, however, be disrupted by a drastic change, or punctuation, that reconfigures the language ecology. A punctuation can result in new languages being formed, existing languages becoming extinct or a particular group and its language increasing its status and influence (Dixon, 1997). There are two aspects to punctuation: its causes and geographical parameters.

Dixon (1997) identifies natural causes, material innovations, development of aggressive tendencies and writing and other forms of communication as the reasons for a punctuation occurring. Natural causes include floods, droughts, volcanoes, changes in sea level and diseases. All of these can cause a reduction in population, changes to the living area or the merging or migration of peoples. Material innovations, such as tools and weapons, can give one group an advantage over others in terms of obtaining resources and resolving conflicts, respectively. Developments in transport allow increased mobility and make it possible for people to explore new areas and access new resources. This applies to both land and water-based transport.

Another cause of punctuation is the development of aggressive tendencies among a group of people. This group may be prompted by political, ideological or religious motivations to seek more power for itself and therefore conquer others. Finally, writing and other forms of communication contribute to a punctuation.[4] This is because writing is generally associated with the language of a group of people who have become more powerful than others through the above means. Little may be published in other languages, and the same applies to the production of radio and television content, meaning other languages have little or no presence in these domains (Dixon, 1997).

All of these factors make one group more powerful than others. In such circumstances, the language of the powerful group gains prestige, and its niche will expand. Other groups will learn the prestige language, but the powerful group will likely not learn the non-prestige languages of other groups.

A punctuation can also occur along three geographical parameters. The first of these is expansion into uninhabited territory, in which a group moves to a new place for any number of reasons (changes in the environment, developments in transport etc.). As a result, it has the advantage of access to large amounts of resources. A punctuation can also occur within a particular geographical area for any of the reasons discussed above. In such cases, the punctuation and its effects are confined to that area. The third possibility is a punctuation involving expansion into a previously occupied area. This is usually an invasion by a group with some material advantage and/or a political, ideological or religious motivation to spread its influence. This group's language becomes the prestige language while other languages in the area either decline in use or at the very least become less important (Dixon, 1997). Once again, such a language will expand its niche at the expense of others.

Drawing on Nettle and Romaine's (2000) work, I map out how the global ecology of languages has been reconfigured by a series of punctuations. These centre on major events in world history, from the development of agriculture through to colonisation, industrialisation and globalisation. I then give special attention to how English obtained its current position in the global language system in relation to such events, before arguing China's rise should also be treated as a punctuation which will, like the others before it, reshape the global ecology of languages.

2.4 LONG-STANDING EQUILIBRIUM

By 10,000 years ago, modern humans and their languages had reached all major continents. Many consider this period to be the height of linguistic diversity, with 10,000–15,000 languages in existence (Evans, 2010; Fischer, 2018; Matthews, 2003). At this stage, all of the world's population were hunter-gatherers. Such societies had certain characteristics that supported equilibrium. Firstly, language groups would have been small, with possibly no more than a few thousand speakers (Nettle & Romaine, 2000). The hunter-gatherer lifestyle also meant establishing dominance would have been difficult because most groups of people were moving around on a regular basis.[5] In addition, dominance would require one group to become significantly larger than the others, which the environment could not support. Another result of this lifestyle was that hunter-gatherers tended to be relatively egalitarian. They had to spend most of their time finding food, and therefore could not be full-time chiefs or politicians. Their interactions and social organisation were limited to their own group and neighbouring groups, which would also have been small (Diamond, 2017). Also working against one group and their language becoming dominant were the difficulties associated with establishing and maintaining control over resources. It was not practical to accumulate a large amount of resources (for example food) as they would have to be carried around (Nettle & Romaine, 2000).

People likely acquired the languages of neighbouring groups for the purposes of interaction, and multilingualism could have been common. In some cases, people may have acquired another group's language because they perceived that group and its situation to be more desirable than their own. However, this would have occurred on a small geographical scale and would have been temporary. As Nettle and Romaine (2000) say, the world at this time lacked "massive, enduring differences between the expansionary potential of different peoples, of the kind which would cause the sustained expansion of a single, dominant language" (p. 100). Because the hunter-gatherer lifestyle lasted for most of humanity's time on earth, the usual state of affairs was most likely equilibrium.

2.5   THE FIRST BIG PUNCTUATION: AGRICULTURE AND ITS CONSEQUENCES

The hunter-gatherer lifestyle that supported equilibrium eventually disappeared following the emergence of agriculture. Between approximately 8500 and 3000 BCE, agriculture developed in southwest Asia, southeast Asia, China and North and South America (Nolan & Lenski, 2015).

Exactly why and how agriculture developed is unknown, especially considering it involved more work than hunter-gathering and initially made people worse off (McNeill & McNeill, 2003). However, it is likely to have developed slowly, and over a long period of time, in response to changes in the environment and human population. According to Diamond (2017), wild food was becoming scarce, population density was rising and plants and animals which could be domesticated were increasingly available. Humans had also developed improved tools and techniques for obtaining and dealing with wild foods, many of which could be applied to agriculture. The hunter-gatherer lifestyle was therefore becoming less rewarding, and there were greater incentives to take up agriculture and/or herding. Under such circumstances, some people turned to growing various kinds of plants and domesticating animals. There were now groups of farmers as well as hunter-gathers.

This had significant consequences, and represents the first big punctuation in the global ecology of languages. Nettle and Romaine (2000) explain that "for perhaps the first time in history, there were now massive differences in the size and density of societies confronting each other over how resources were to be shared" (p. 108). In any such confrontations, it was farmers who had the advantage. Firstly, farming led to population growth. Farmers could choose to grow the kinds of plants that were most useful as food sources, and in this way, a given area of land could produce much more food through farming than hunting and gathering.

More food meant it was possible to support more people, and the population increased. Animals also contributed to an increase in population. Not only were they a source of food—in the form of meat, milk and milk products like cheese and yoghurt—but they also helped to produce more food by tilling land that humans could not on their own, and producing manure which could be used as fertiliser to increase crop yields. Once again, more food meant more people. Equally important was that animals such as horses, cows and camels could be used to transport people and their possessions over long distances, thus allowing farming groups to spread (Diamond, 2017).

Farming also resulted in a sedentary lifestyle, and this meant children could be born at shorter intervals. A hunter-gatherer can only carry one child and must wait until that child can walk before having another, but this is not the case for sedentary farmers. Farmers were therefore numerically stronger than hunter-gatherers (Morris, 2011).

Farmers had other advantages beyond weight of numbers. Remaining in one place meant food could be stored, and this in turn freed some people from involvement in food production. They could then specialise in other roles, such as chiefs/rulers, priests and soldiers, on a full-time basis. This resulted in firmer social organisation and hierarchy in farming groups than in hunter-gatherer groups (Diamond, 2017).

Farming also required more land, meaning farmers spread, taking their languages with them. The Indo-European, Elamo-Dravidian, Sino-Tibetan, Austroasiatic and Bantu language families, for example, were all associated with places where agriculture developed, and spread over large areas. Hunter-gatherers were forced into marginal areas or had to take up farming, and in this way the languages used by farmers spread over greater areas at the expense of those used by hunter-gatherers. The spread of farming, and by implication the languages associated with it, stopped only where the environment was not suitable or where natural barriers such as mountains prevented it going further (Nettle & Romaine, 2000).

While agriculture certainly created a major change in the global ecology of languages, equilibrium did reemerge. Farming groups were larger than hunter-gather ones, but probably had a maximum size of several ten thousands, and their political structures remained relatively loose. Consequently, such groups fragmented as they spread, and their languages evolved in different directions (Evans, 2010; Nettle & Romaine, 2000).

2.6   THE PUNCTUATION
SPREADS: EUROPEAN EXPANSION

Farming was most prominent in Eurasia because of the availability of plant and animal species suited to domestication. This put Eurasian peoples in an advantageous position because of the effects of farming on population, technology, social organisation and disease (Diamond, 2017; Nettle & Romaine, 2000).

The population of Eurasia grew rapidly while that of other continents stayed relatively stable. With a larger population, it was necessary to develop technological and administrative innovations to continue to produce food, manage the population and resolve conflicts with other groups. These included, over time, weapons, bureaucracy and writing. All this meant that Eurasians were "better armed and more hierarchically controlled" than peoples in other areas of the world (Nettle & Romaine, 2000, p. 113).

Eurasians lived close together and also lived close to livestock, which supported diseases. Measles, smallpox, tuberculosis and influenza all originated in Eurasia, and this gave Eurasians some resistance to these diseases (McNeill & McNeill, 2003). These factors would have significant consequences for languages when Eurasians spread to other parts of the world. As Karttunen and Crosby (1995) point out, "it is a good rule of thumb that the advance of civilization – that is the expansion of mobile, densely populated, technologically adept societies, often hierarchically organized – brings about a reduction in the number of languages" (p. 159).

From 1500 to 1800, Europe became the most powerful region in the world, surpassing Asia and the Middle East, which until that point had equal or higher levels of agriculture, technology and social organisation.[6] Europe was therefore in a position to expand its influence over the rest of the world as a result. The fifteenth and sixteenth centuries marked the beginnings of European voyages of exploration which resulted in the establishment of trading posts and then colonies in Africa, Asia, the Americas and the Pacific. This was, according to Nettle and Romaine (2000), a continuation of the first punctuation in that groups of people who possessed agriculture, technology, social organisation and diseases destroyed or displaced those who did not. Indigenous peoples and their languages were devastated through colonisation. For example, at the time of European settlement in Australia in 1788, over 250 Indigenous languages were spoken. Today, only 13 of these are still being acquired by children, and approximately another 100 are spoken only by older generations, and remain at risk of extinction (Australian Institute of Aboriginal and Torres Strait Islander Studies, 2019). Unlike the previous punctuation, the groups and languages that spread with it did not diverge to any great extent because Europeans "were tied together by modern communication, writing, and states" (Nettle & Romaine, 2000, pp. 124–125). Languages such as English, French, Portuguese, Spanish and Dutch were spread around the world during this period (Ostler, 2011).

Nevertheless, the European expansion could only go as far as the environment and geography would allow. The climate had to suit European crops and animals, and there had to be enough space in which to live and set up farms. Tropical Africa, the southeast Asian islands, New Guinea and some Pacific Islands remained relatively undisturbed by this expanding punctuation in the global ecology of languages (Nettle & Romaine, 2000).

2.7   THE NEXT BIG PUNCTUATION: INDUSTRIALISATION AND ITS CONSEQUENCES

The type of language spread associated with the punctuations discussed so far has two characteristics. Firstly, it involved the movement of people—farmers taking more land and Europeans colonising various parts of the world. Secondly, the spread of languages was constrained by geography and the environment. The next big punctuation was different in that it did not involve the large-scale movement of people. Instead, groups of people switched from using their own languages to the language of a more powerful group, at least for some purposes, without speakers of that language being physically present. In other words, this punctuation was a case of language shift, and as such it could go beyond the constraints of the previous one (Nettle & Romaine, 2000; Ostler, 2011).

The decisive factor in this punctuation was economic transformation, culminating in the Industrial Revolution of the eighteenth century, and its subsequent effects on the world (Kottak, 2016; Nettle & Romaine, 2000). Prior to the Industrial Revolution, people were dependent on the land for food, clothing, shelter and fuel. The Industrial Revolution changed this by bringing about a shift to "the manufacture of goods in a factory and by a machine, for sale outside the neighbourhood concerned" (Simmons, 1996, p. 208).

The Industrial Revolution was sparked by population growth, availability of resources such as coal and availability of capital to invest in technological development. It resulted in greater levels of production, new technologies and higher (although unevenly spread) standards of living (Kottak, 2016; Marks, 2015). The Industrial Revolution happened first in England, and by the end of the nineteenth century the main industrialised areas of the world were Europe, Russia, the USA and Japan (Simmons, 1996).

Other countries were drawn into relationships with industrialised countries, either by being brought under their influence or by attempting to industrialise themselves (McNeill & McNeill, 2003). It is this socioeconomic integration that caused language shift because it required knowledge of certain languages to participate in or interact with more powerful industrialised societies and/or to gain the benefits of industrialisation, such as goods, services and employment (Evans, 2010; Mufwene, 2001).

Given the pattern of industrialisation, it was mainly European languages that came to be associated with economic development and modernisation. These languages were therefore acquired by others. This was not of course entirely a matter of free choice. The benefits of industrialisation were certainly appealing, and would have led people to acquire the languages associated with it. But the spread of industrialisation, like the spread of farming, was the result of asymmetries of power between groups. Members of the less powerful groups did not create the conditions which made European languages important and were not in a position to define what choices were available or feasible (Nettle & Romaine, 2000).

2.8   THE PUNCTUATION SPREADS AGAIN: GLOBALISATION AND ITS CONSEQUENCES

The same dynamic operates today, but on a larger scale, due to the processes of globalisation. Globalisation can be defined as "the multiplicity of linkages and interconnections that transcend the nation states (and by implication the societies) which make up the modern world system" (McGrew, 1992, p. 65). Interconnections across the world are by no means new—as the above discussion demonstrates—but they have increased and intensified in recent decades. These interconnections imply a reorganisation of the world and the way we act in it, which goes beyond the immediate, local, physical location. In other words, relations among people, states, organisations etc. have become substantially deterritorialised (Scholte, 2005).

Such deterritorialised connections among the various actors in the world mean communication must take place across national, cultural and linguistic boundaries, and this in turn requires the acquisition and use of languages (Piller & Grey, 2019). For example, transnational corporations (TNCs) operate across the borders of nation states, and many adopt a common language for communications within their own organisations and with other organisations. Nation states have alliances with each other and also join international organisations such as the United Nations (UN), North Atlantic Treaty Organisation (NATO) and Africa Union (AU) to ensure their own security. A common language is essential for the effective conduct of military operations. Discussions and negotiations about issues such as climate change, which go beyond national borders, are also facilitated by language. Meanwhile, computer and Internet technology have made information more easily available and not limited to national media outlets. Accessing this information requires learning the languages in which it is produced (Wright, 2016). The power of a language is then determined by the linkages that can be made with it, that is the people and resources which can be accessed through the language.

Globalisation therefore impacts on people's linguistic repertoires because they need to acquire the languages which can be used to make the greatest number of connections (Kroon et al., 2014). This has placed additional demands on those who do not already speak one of these languages. For example, the Saami people of Scandinavia already need to acquire a central language (Swedish, Norwegian or Finnish depending on the state they reside in) in addition to Saami, and a supercentral language or hypercentral English if they wish to communicate internationally (Nettle & Romaine, 2000). Similarly, members of the Zhuang ethnic minority in China need to acquire Mandarin for socioeconomic mobility on the national level, and English for socioeconomic mobility globally (Grey & Piller, 2020). The niches of central, supercentral and the hypercentral language are expanded, while those of peripheral languages are further reduced. These languages may also be perceived as lacking value or utility, and may not be passed on to future generations.

Globalisation has thus consolidated and expanded the position of already powerful languages because it was driven primarily by Western countries and actors associated with them (Grey & Piller, 2020). As the above examples allude to, this is most obvious in the case of English. The way English connects to the punctuations discussed above deserves particular attention in this discussion of the global ecology of languages.

2.9   HOW ENGLISH BECOME A GLOBAL LANGUAGE

Leith and Seargeant (2012) argue that "the global spread of English begun within the British Isles" (p. 112). From 43 to 410 CE, Britain was a Roman province where Latin was the language of government and was used by Roman military personnel, civilian officials and settlers. The native population spoke the Celtic languages of British, Cornish, Irish and Scots Gaelic, and some would also have used Latin for interacting with the Romans. English began as the dialects spoken by Germanic tribes, namely the Angles, Saxons and Jutes.[7] These dialects arrived in Britain when, following the withdrawal of the Roman legions, the Celts invited Germanic mercenaries to help protect them from Vikings and hostile Celtic tribes from the north of Britain and Ireland (Fennell, 2001; Freeborn, 2006).

These Germanic peoples instead conquered what is now England and divided it into seven kingdoms: Northumbria, Mercia, East Anglia, Essex, Kent, Sussex and Wessex. Three dialects of English were spoken within these kingdoms, namely Anglian, Kentish and West Saxon. Anglian was made up of Northumbrian and Mercian spoken by the Angles, and both Kentish and West Saxon came from the dialects of the Saxons and Jutes (Freeborn, 2006; Minkova & Stockwell, 2009). With the Celts driven into marginal areas or forced into servitude, English became the dominant language and continued developing through a number of influences.

One of these was conversion to Christianity. Roman missionaries led by Augustine came to Britain in 597 CE, bringing with them Latin. Latin became the language of religion and other important functions, while English served as the language of everyday life. Latin influenced and elaborated English lexis, morphology and syntax, and some loan words from Greek also came into English through Christianity (Crystal, 2002; Svartvik & Leech, 2006). From the eighth century until the eleventh century, Viking raids occurred, and at one stage Vikings controlled part of Britain, known as the Danelaw. The Danelaw incorporated Northumbria, southeast Scotland and some of eastern Mercia, bringing English into contact with Scandinavian languages. While these languages never displaced English, English was influenced by them, most notably in terms of loan words pertaining to place names and surnames (Freeborn, 2006). The next significant event in the history of English was the Norman Conquest of 1066. This resulted in "the abolition of the entire political, economic, and cultural infrastructure of Anglo-Saxon England" (Leitner, 1992, p. 189). French was imposed on the country and, for the next three centuries, was the language of law, government and administration, and to a lesser extent religion. The strict social separation between the French-speaking nobility and English-speaking peasantry and lower classes meant bilingualism was not widespread. However, many French words found their way into English, including those pertaining to administration, the military, education and the arts. English reemerged as the dominant language when tensions between the French and English resulted in the Normans losing their holdings in Normandy and ultimately severing contacts with the French altogether. The Normans eventually assimilated to English society and English was re-established in the domains previously dominated by French. For example, in the early 1360s, English took over from French and Latin in Parliament and the courts (Minkova & Stockwell, 2009; Northrup, 2013).

The reemergence of English overlaps roughly with the Renaissance, a time of new ideas, new inventions and exploration. It was in this climate that English, particularly the London dialect, was gaining new respect among the educated and professionals, and undergoing standardisation, which encouraged its use in printing, government communication and mass communication (Freeborn, 2006; Leitner, 1992). Eventually, as a result of English political and economic power, government policy (especially in education) and prevailing attitudes towards other languages, English was well-established throughout the British Isles (Leith, 1997). However, as English lacked the vocabulary to discuss the new ideas of the time, it borrowed from other languages. From Greek and Latin came words for scientific and medical terms, and from Italian, Dutch, Spanish and Portuguese came words pertaining to many aspects of life, including food, music and clothing. English speakers were also spreading to the New World, and borrowed words from various African, Asian and Native American languages (Minkova & Stockwell, 2009). Even among English speakers the language was considered inferior to others, and the idea that it would have any global function "was regarded as absurd" (Bailey, 1992, p. 96).

An important factor in making English a global language was British colonialism. Motivated by the need to find new resources, political rivalries and the desire for wealth, Britain colonised various African, Asian and Pacific countries (Schneider, 2011). At its height, the British Empire covered a fifth of the earth's land surface and a quarter of its population (Kottak, 2016).

Colonialism established English in many parts of the world, although in different ways depending on the nature of the colony. There were three types of colony: (i) those in which large numbers of English speakers settled and displaced the pre-colonial population, such as occurred in Australia and America; (ii) those in which a small number of English speakers settled and administered and controlled the pre-colonial population, allowing some to learn English, such as occurred in Nigeria, India and Cameroon; and (iii) those in which the pre-colonial population was replaced by a labour force of slaves from somewhere else, usually Africa, such as occurred in Barbados and Jamaica. In the first type of colony, English became the predominant native language at the expense of the indigenous languages. In the second type, it became the language of administration and sometimes the medium of instruction in education. In such cases English was used as a second or additional language alongside indigenous languages. The third type of colony resulted in English-based pidgins and creoles because English facilitated communication among African slaves from diverse linguistic backgrounds. Over generations, these pidgins and creoles developed into native varieties of English (Galloway & Rose, 2015; Leith & Seargeant, 2012).

English also provided material rewards and opportunities to those able to speak it during the colonial era. Firstly, knowledge of English was a means of obtaining employment in the colonial administration as a clerk, translator, interpreter or servant. Secondly, English sometimes became a lingua franca for use among the linguistically diverse peoples in the colonies. After gaining independence, many former colonies kept English as an official language because choosing an indigenous language for this role could lead to conflict among different groups. English, on the other hand, was often seen as neutral because it did not favour one group's language over another's (Blake, 1996; Leith, 1997).

Another important factor in making English a global language was the Industrial Revolution, which first took place in Britain. English was therefore the language most closely associated with the emerging new developments and technology, and anyone who wanted to learn about them had to learn English in order to access the related information and literature, and pursue research and development. Many countries dispatched missions of inquiry to Britain or seconded workers to its factories (Crystal, 2003). Inventors and scholars from other countries also came to Britain to further their work. One such example was William Siemens, who travelled from Germany to Britain to find investors and manufacturers for his family's inventions, and needed to acquire English in order to do so (Wright, 2016). Some of the new technology of the time, such as the telegraph and telephone, further contributed to the spread of English by creating a far-reaching communications network largely dominated by English (Crystal, 2003; Fennell, 2001).

Other languages, such as French, Portuguese, Dutch and Spanish, were also spread around the world via colonialism, and their countries of origin underwent industrialisation. However, the use and status of these languages globally declined, at least to some degree, along with the empires with which they were associated (Graddol, 1997). This did not happen in the case of English, because it was also the language of America, which would have a very important role in the world. By the end of the nineteenth century, America had become the fastest growing economy in the world and had taken over from Britain as the world's leading industrial and trading nation. The scientific and technological developments of the Industrial Revolution were continued and expanded by American inventors and researchers, such as Thomas Edison, Samuel Morse and Robert Fulton. Inventors and scholars from other parts of the world were attracted to America to pursue their work and learn about new scientific and technological developments, as they had been drawn to England earlier on (Crystal, 2003).

America's involvement in World War II "introduced many parts of the world to US people, language and consumer goods" (Graddol, 2007, p. 248). More important for making English a global language however, was America's role in shaping the international system after the war. This included establishing international organisations like the United Nations (UN) and the International Monetary Fund (IMF), and sponsoring re-development through the Marshall Plan, all of which functioned at least partly through English. During the Cold War between America and the Soviet Union, America was the leader of the Western world, making English the dominant language of half the Cold War international system, while Russian was the dominant language of the other half. English's association with the modernity and prosperity America represented, as well as its ideals of freedom and democracy, further enhanced its appeal (Graddol, 1997; Wright, 2016).

Following the end of the Cold War and the collapse of the Soviet Union, America was left as the world's sole superpower. Many formerly communist countries attempted to introduce Western ideas, approaches and technologies, which necessitated the learning of English (Blake, 1996; Crystal, 2003). English largely replaced Russian as the priority foreign language in these countries' education systems. Citing official data, Northrup (2013) says that at least 80% of secondary school students in Estonia, Poland, Romania and Slovenia, and over 60% of secondary school students in Bulgaria and the Czech Republic, were studying English by the end of the 1990s.

America has continued to be the world's leader in science and technology, and as such English is linked to many developments which have shaped modern society. One of these is information and communication technologies (ICTs), especially computers and the Internet. Microsoft and Apple were responsible for most of the hardware and software that underpins the information technology revolution. Other American companies such as Genentech and Amgen produced important advances and innovations in biotechnology, while Pfizer and Merck, Sharpe and Dohme did the same in pharmaceuticals, and Motorola, Loral Space and Communications and Teledisc did so in satellite telecommunications infrastructure (Wright, 2016).

Equally important to making English a global language was America's cultural influence. From approximately the middle of the nineteenth century onwards, many aspects of cultural life were created or further developed in America. These include the press, broadcasting, sound recording and motion pictures. For example, the news agency New York Associated Press was founded in 1856, the first recording company, Columbia, was established in 1898, and the first commercial radio station commenced broadcasts in Pittsburgh, Pennsylvania, in 1920. The film industry was largely based in Hollywood from 1915, where it developed its main characteristics such as the feature film and movie stars. The songwriters and music publishers of New York City, collectively known as Tin Pan Alley, were a significant influence on popular music in the late nineteenth and early twentieth centuries, as were American rock and pop musicians during the mid-twentieth century (Crystal, 2012). Today, many of the most prevalent aspects of popular culture, such as Hollywood blockbusters, television programmes, rap and hip-hop music and video games, likewise originate in America. English is appealing as the means to access these aspects of popular culture for personal enjoyment, especially for young people. It can also be an avenue for the creation of new popular culture artefacts, whether in English, other languages or a mixture of both (McKay, 2002).

2.10   The Punctuation Shifts: China's Rise

According to Dixon (1997), the current punctuation was "still in mid-stream" (p. 67) and equilibrium had not returned at the time he wrote his book. This remains the case today, although I argue that in the intervening years, this punctuation has changed. Until recently it had mainly been Western countries—Europe and the USA—that shaped the way the modern world operates, and this made their languages powerful and prestigious, especially English. However, as the centre of world power has shifted towards Asia, and China in particular, the force behind the punctuation is also shifting.

In the late 1970s, China commenced a programme of reform and opening up (改革开放 *gǎigé kāifàng*) to modernise and develop the country. The Four Modernisations, as this programme was known, focused on agriculture, industry, national defence and science and technology. It was accompanied by a loosening of state control of the economy and society in aid of this goal. While certainly not without its problems, reform and opening up achieved some notable successes, including spectacular economic growth, improvements in living standards and greater connectivity with the rest of the world (Shambaugh, 2020).

Since the 2000s, China has sought to take a greater and more proactive role in the world through its "going global" (走出去 *zǒu chūqù*) strategy. Going Global has a number of elements, including securing energy resources; encouraging Chinese companies to invest in and purchase assets; promoting Chinese culture; and creating an international media presence, all beyond China's borders. This strategy was intended to enhance the modernisation and development begun with the Four Modernisations, and create an international environment favourable for China (Zhang, 2012).

Many of these initiatives have continued under current president Xi Jinping, and have been incorporated into the goal of achieving the Chinese Dream (中国梦 *zhōngguó mèng*) of the Great Rejuvenation (大复

兴 *dà fùxīng*) of China into the world's most powerful country. Domestically, the means of achieving the Chinese Dream include the centralisation of authority under Xi Jinping himself, reassertion of state influence in the economy and society and restriction of foreign influence and competition in the economy and society. Internationally, the Chinese Dream is being pursued through the promotion of Chinese culture, ideas and narratives; efforts to reshape global norms and institutions; and greater projection of China's power on the global stage (Economy, 2018; Shambaugh, 2020).

Whether the Chinese Dream becomes a reality remains to be seen, but there is no doubt that China is now an increasingly important "pole in the global geopolitical, economic and cultural order" (Grey & Piller, 2020, p. 55), and a rising global power which "is now deeply embedded on every continent and in every society" (Shambaugh, 2020, p. 4). Based on the previous punctuations, this will mean Chinese becomes associated with various forms of power and becomes increasingly desirable to acquire and use. As we saw in Chapter 1, this has already started to occur in the form of Chinese fever. The following two chapters will deal with this in depth. For now though, a framework for defining and describing the forms of power that drive macroacquisition is required.

2.11   Language Comprehensive Competitiveness: Definition and Background

When languages are associated with resources, they have power in a language ecology, whether it be on a local, national or global level. Other scholars have explored this before, usually from the perspective of language as a kind of capital (see, for example, Park & Wee, 2012; Norton, 2000; Norton & Gao, 2008; Norton Peirce, 1995; Zhou, 2019). However, these previous works did not define and describe the resources which give a language power. The language comprehensive competitiveness (语言综合竞争力 *yǔyán zōnghé jìngzhēng lì*) framework can be used for this purpose.

Language comprehensive competitiveness was first developed by Zou and You (2001) to analyse the use and status of languages and dialects in multilingual societies. In line with the notion of a competitive language ecology discussed earlier in this chapter, they argue that when more than one language or dialect is used in the same society or community, three kinds of competition can eventuate: (i) which language or dialect will function as the high variety and which as the low variety;

(ii) which domains each language or dialect will be used in, for example schools, media and public transport; and (iii) which language or dialect will borrow words from the other(s). The outcome of these issues will be determined by each language's or dialect's language comprehensive competitiveness (Zou & You, 2001). Zou and You (2001) discuss how this applies to the language ecologies of Hong Kong, Taiwan, mainland China and Singapore.

Later, Xu (2007) expanded the application of language comprehensive competitiveness to the use and status of languages on the global level. She focuses primarily on Chinese and English, although her analysis is somewhat brief with a short discussion of each component of language comprehensive competitiveness and its connection to global language status. Her work provides a useful starting point for a fuller investigation of the macroacquisition of Chinese and its implications. Interestingly, neither Zou and You (2001) nor Xu (2007) provide a definition of language comprehensive competitiveness. In line with what has been discussed in this chapter, I define it as the association of a language with forms of power and resources that are valuable and bring benefits to speakers of the language within a language ecology.

2.12 Components of Language Comprehensive Competitiveness

In its original version, language comprehensive competitiveness consisted of five components: political competitiveness, cultural competitiveness, economic competitiveness, population competitiveness and script competitiveness. Political competitiveness refers to the extent to which governments and international organisations emphasise the use of the language and promote it through their language planning and language policy (Xu, 2007; Zou & You, 2001). I rename this policy competitiveness as this more aptly reflects its definition. Policy competitiveness is clearly important as it ensures a language has presence in an ecology. Zhou (2019) also points out that the policies of local and national governments, as well as international organisations, influence a language's association with other kinds of power and resources.

Cultural competitiveness refers to the vitality, prestige and popularity of the traditional and contemporary culture associated with the language, such as classic works of philosophy, literature and art, and contemporary movies, television programmes, news, literature and art (Xu, 2007; Zou &

You, 2001). This component of language comprehensive competitiveness is important because it means a language is a vehicle to access high and popular cultural products, and thus gives it cultural influence.

Economic competitiveness refers to the level of economic development and economic power of the area in which the language is spoken, while population competitiveness refers to the number of people who speak a language and the number of people who learn it as a second/additional language (Xu, 2007; Zou & You, 2001). Economic power is perhaps the most salient form of power in today's world, and means a language is associated with trade, business and employment. Population competitiveness means a language can be used to connect and communicate with other people.

Finally, script competitiveness refers to whether a language has a written script and the quality of this script (Xu, 2007). A written script is necessary for a language to be used for important purposes such as literacy and education, and allows professional and general communication to occur across time and space. A written script is also a necessity for the use of a language in print media and on the Internet (Montgomery, 2013). In this sense, a written script allows a language to be used in more domains than would otherwise be possible.

2.13   ADDITIONS TO THE LANGUAGE COMPREHENSIVE COMPETITIVENESS FRAMEWORK

I propose that three more components need to be added to this framework: scientific/technological competitiveness, educational competitiveness and geostrategic competitiveness. Scientific/technological competitiveness is a necessary addition because science and technology are widely acknowledged to play an important role in today's world. For example, the invention of new things and the refinement and adaptation of existing things are essential to a country's ability to enhance the standard of living of its population, compete with other countries, increase its independence, and become attractive to others (Lampton, 2008). An association with science and technology has also been shown to encourage the macroacquisition of a language, as in the case of the close association of English with the Industrial Revolution in Britain and the later invention of many modern technologies in the USA. I therefore define scientific/technological competitiveness as new developments and advances in the fields of science and technology in the area where the language is spoken, and the utility of the language as a means to access information about such advances and developments.

Similarly, I argue educational competitiveness is a necessary addition because education can bring a country a range of benefits, including increased living standards, a skilled workforce and attractiveness to others. Scholarly research activities can also generate new ideas and concepts (Lampton, 2008). This can prompt the macroacquisition of the language in which education and research are undertaken, as others seek to access new philosophies, ideas and concepts. For example, English is currently learnt to access research in a wide range of fields (Wright, 2016). Educational competitiveness, as I define it, thus refers to the quality of education, especially higher education, and scholarly research in the area where the language is spoken, and the utility of the language to access education and research.

Finally, the results of a previous study I conducted (Gil, 2014) suggest China's importance in the world is encouraging people to learn Chinese. Because of this, I also add a component called geostrategic competitiveness to the language comprehensive competitiveness framework. I define geostrategic competitiveness as the extent of the interests of the country (or countries) where the language is spoken in the international system, and its influence within the international system.

Language comprehensive competitiveness offers a useful framework for investigating the macroacquisition of Chinese because we can assume that some of its components will support macroacquisition, while others will constrain it. Identifying the role of each component will produce a language comprehensive competitiveness profile of Chinese within the global ecology of languages.

2.14   Sources and Methods for Investigating Language Comprehensive Competitiveness and Some Limitations

As explained in Chapter 1, two perspectives on which components of language comprehensive competitiveness support or constrain macroacquisition are required: the objective perspective and the subjective perspective. This fits well with the global ecology of languages approach articulated in this chapter because, as Hornberger and Hult (2008) explain, a language ecology has both a sociological and psychological aspect. That is, there is the objective situation of a language within the ecology, and the subjective views of the language and its situation held by people.

In this book, the sociological aspect is covered by the objective perspective. It refers to the niche of Chinese, that is, the current standing, uses and resources available in and through Chinese. As such, it is concerned with how language practices and language management demonstrate the association of Chinese with various forms of power and resources as represented in the components of language comprehensive competitiveness. The subjective perspective covers the psychological aspect of a language ecology. It is concerned with how people perceive or view Chinese, that is their language beliefs/ideology. It refers to people's perceptions, ideas and beliefs about the association of Chinese with various forms of power and resources as represented in the components of language comprehensive competitiveness.

To explore the macroacquisition of Chinese from the objective perspective, I conducted a secondary analysis of existing data. According to Blaxter et al. (2010), a secondary analysis of existing data involves the researcher analysing written, online, archived or visual materials from the perspective of his or her research questions. I looked for data relevant to each of the components of language comprehensive competitiveness from various sources which contained useful and readily accessible data: media documents (print and online newspaper reports regarding the use of Chinese in various domains and the learning of Chinese), websites of various organisations (policies regarding language use and comparative information on China and other Chinese-speaking areas), and government surveys and reports (language use surveys and statistical compilations regarding China and other Chinese-speaking areas).

In addition, I also drew on academic sources including journal articles, book chapters and books in the fields of linguistics, applied linguistics and sociolinguistics. Where possible and appropriate, I drew comparisons to English. This is because English is the clearest case of the global macroacquisitionof a language and therefore offers a yardstick for investigating the macroacquisition of other languages from the objective perspective.

To explore the macroacquisition of Chinese from the subjective perspective, I collected new data through a survey of and interviews with Chinese language learners, interviews with Chinese language teachers and interviews with Chinese scholars. 75 Chinese language learners from universities in Australia and China completed the survey. Nine of these also completed follow-up email interviews. As for Chinese language teachers, a total of 30 from universities in Australia and China completed interviews either via email or in person. Three interviews I conducted with Chinese scholars at a research institute in China also formed part of the data for investigating the subjective perspective of the macroacquisitionof Chinese.[8] I chose Australia and China as the research sites because these are the contexts with which I am familiar, and to which I have access through my professional connections.

Two limitations need to be noted. First of all, my study of the language comprehensive competitiveness of Chinese is cross-sectional. This means it provides "a snapshot-like analysis of the target phenomenon at one particular point in time, focusing on a single time interval" (Dörnyei, 2007, p. 78). It does not capture changes or developments over time. To overcome this, I have endeavoured to ensure the information I used throughout the book is as current as possible.

Secondly, because my findings regarding the subjective perspective on the language comprehensive competitiveness of Chinese are based on a small number of participants from universities in Australia and China, their generalisability might be regarded as somewhat limited. I would make two points in response to this. Firstly, the data has analytic generalisability (Blommaert & Dong, 2010; Dörnyei, 2007; Duff, 2008) in the sense that it provides insights into how the macroacquisition of Chinese works from the subjective perspective, and these insights can then be applied in other contexts. Secondly, participants—particularly the Chinese language learners—were from diverse backgrounds and were drawn from different countries, universities, and learning environments. As Duff (2006, 2008) suggests, the presence of common patterns in data gathered across diverse circumstances such as these increases their generalisability.[9] I believe this is an appropriate and achievable expectation for a book of this size and scope.

2.15 Conclusion

This chapter established the book's conceptual framework by setting the macroacquisition of Chinese within the global ecology of languages. Within this approach, China's rise can be regarded as a punctuation which will have important consequences for the learning and use of second/additional languages, manifested in the phenomenon of Chinese fever. I have shown how an expanded version of language comprehensive competitiveness provides a useful tool for investigating the macroacquisition of Chinese because it identifies the various resources which make a language important. The following chapters demonstrate which components of language comprehensive competitiveness support or constrain the macroacquisition of Chinese, and explore the consequences of this for the future of English as a global language.

NOTES

1. Although there were earlier uses of the "ecology of language" or similar terms, Haugen is generally regarded as the founder of this approach. See Eliasson (2015) for further discussion.
2. The scale of a language ecology can range from "social groups to classrooms to schools to cities to regions to countries and beyond" (Hult, 2013). My focus in this book is on the global level, but I acknowledge that the global language ecology is underpinned by many other language ecologies at various scales.
3. The notion of punctuated equilibrium was first developed by Stephen Jay Gould in 1967 to explain evolution. It has since been used in various fields.
4. Dixon (1997) identifies writing and other forms of communication as a "strong concomitant factor" rather than a cause of punctuation in and of themselves (p. 80).
5. Some hunter-gather groups were sedentary, such as those of the Pacific Northwest of the USA (Nettle & Romaine, 2000).
6. The reasons for this are complex and beyond the scope of this book. Detailed discussion can be found in Kupchan (2012), Morris (2011), and Pomeranz (2000).
7. At a purely linguistic level, English has undergone substantial changes in grammar, vocabulary, pronunciation and semantics throughout its history. These are not dealt with in this book. Interested readers should consult Blake (1996), Fennell (2001), and Minkova and Stockwell (2009).
8. I provide further details about the participants and how they were recruited in Chapter 4.
9. I discuss how these limitations could be addressed in further research in Chapter 8.

REFERENCES

Australian Institute of Aboriginal and Torres Strait Islander Studies. (2019). *Indigenous Australian languages*. Retrieved 21 January 2020, from https:// aiatsis.gov.au/explore/articles/indigenous-australian-languages

Bailey, R. W. (1992). *Images of English: A cultural history of the language.* Cambridge University Press.

Blake, N. F. (1996). *A history of the English language.* Macmillan Press.

Blaxter, L., Hughes, C., & Tight, M. (2010). *How to research* (4th ed.). Open University Press McGraw-Hill Education.

Blommaert, J., & Dong, J. (2010). *Ethnographic fieldwork: A beginner's guide.* Multilingual Matters.

Calvet, L. J. (2006). *Towards an ecology of world languages* (A. Brown, Trans.). Polity (Original work published 1999).

Crystal, D. (2002). *The English language: A guided tour of the language* (2nd ed.). Penguin Books.

Crystal, D. (2003). *English as a global language* (2nd ed.). Cambridge University Press.

Crystal, D. (2012). A global language. In P. Seargeant & J. Swann (Eds.), *English in the world: History, diversity, change* (pp. 151–196). Routledge and The Open University.

Diamond, J. (2017). *Guns, germs, and steel: A short history of everybody for the last 13,000 years.* Vintage.

Dixon, R. M. W. (1997). *The rise and fall of languages.* Cambridge University Press.

Dörnyei, Z. (2007). *Research methods in applied linguistics: Quantitative, qualitative, and mixed methodologies.* Oxford University Press.

Duff, P. A. (2006). Beyond generalizability: Contextualization, complexity, and credibility in applied linguistics research. In M. Chalhoub-Deville, C.A. Chapelle, & P. Duff (Eds.), *Inference and generalizability in applied linguistics: Multiple perspectives* (pp. 65-95). John Benjamins Publishing Company.

Duff, P. A. (2008). *Case study research in applied linguistics.* Lawrence Erlbaum Associates.

Economy, E. C. (2018). *The third revolution: Xi Jinping and the new Chinese state.* Oxford University Press.

Eliasson, S. (2015). The birth of language ecology: Interdisciplinary influences in Einar Haugen's "The ecology of language." *Language Sciences, 50,* 78–92.

Evans, N. (2010). *Dying words: Endangered languages and what they have to tell us.* Wiley-Blackwell.

Fennell, B. A. (2001). *A history of English: A sociolinguistic approach.* Blackwell.

Fischer, S. R. (2018). *A history of language* (New). . Reaktion Books.

Freeborn, D. (2006). *From Old English to Standard English: A course book in language variation across time* (3rd ed.). Palgrave Macmillan.

Galloway, N., & Rose, H. (2015). *Introducing global Englishes.* Routledge.

Gil, J. (2014). An exploratory study of why language learners opt for Chinese and its competitiveness as a world language. *Journal of the Chinese Language Teachers Association, 49*(1), 51–93.

Graddol, D. (1997). *The future of English?* The British Council.
Graddol, D. (2007). Global English, global culture? In S. Goodman, D. Graddol, & T. Lillis (Eds.), *Redesigning English* (2nd ed., pp. 243–279). Routledge and The Open University.
Grenoble, L. (2011). Language ecology and endangerment. In P. K. Austin & J. Sallabank (Eds.), *The Cambridge handbook of endangered languages* (pp. 27–44). Cambridge University Press.
Grey, A., & Piller, I. (2020). Sociolinguistic ethnographies of globalisation. In K. Tusting (Ed.), *The Routledge handbook of linguistic ethnography* (pp. 54–69). Routledge.
Haugen, E. (1972). The ecology of language. In A. S. Dil (Ed.), *The ecology of language: Essays by Einar Haugen* (pp. 325–339). Stanford University Press.
Hornberger, N. H. & Hult, F. M. (2008). Ecological language education policy. In B. Spolsky & F. M. Hult (Eds.), *The handbook of educational linguistics* (pp. 280–296). Blackwell.
Hult, F. M. (2013). Ecology and multilingual education. In C. Chapelle (Ed.), *The encyclopedia of applied linguistics*. Retrieved from Wiley Online Library. https://onlinelibrary.wiley.com/doi/epdf/10.1002/978140 5198431.wbeal0354
Karttunen, F., & Crosby, A. W. (1995). Language death, language genesis, and world history. *Journal of World History, 6*(2), 153–174.
Kottak, C. P. (2016). *Mirror for humanity: A concise introduction to cultural anthropology* (10th ed.). McGraw-Hill Education.
Kroon, S., Blommaert, J., & Dong, J. (2014). *Chinese and globalization* (Tilburg Papers in Culture Studies, No. 111). Retrieved 11 February 2020, from https://pure.uvt.nl/ws/portalfiles/portal/30479973/ TPCS_111_Kroon_Blommaert_Dong.pdf
Kupchan, C. A. (2012). *No one's world: The West, the rising rest, and the coming global turn.* Oxford University Press.
Lampton, D. M. (2008). *The three faces of Chinese power: Might, money and minds.* University of California Press.
Leith, D. (1997). *A social history of English* (2nd ed.). Routledge.
Leith, D., & Seargeant, P. (2012). A colonial language. In P. Seargeant & J. Swann (Eds.), *English in the world: History, diversity, change* (pp. 101–149). Routledge and The Open University.
Leitner, G. (1992). English as a pluricentric language. In M. Clyne (Ed.), *Pluricentric languages: Differing norms in different nations* (pp. 179–237). Mouton de Gruyter.
Marks, R. B. (2015). *The origins of the modern world: A global and ecological narrative from the fifteenth to the twenty-first century* (3rd ed.). Rowman & Littlefield Publishers.

Matthews, S. (2003). The development and spread of languages. In B. Comrie, S. Matthews, & M. Polinksy (Eds.), *SBS atlas of languages: The origin and development of languages throughout the world* (pp. 16–35). ABC Books.

McGrew, A. (1992). A global society? In S. Hall, D. Held, & A. McGrew (Eds.), *Modernity and its futures* (pp. 61–116). Polity Press.

McKay, S. (2002). *Teaching English as an international language: Rethinking goals and approaches*. Oxford University Press.

McNeill, J. R., & McNeill, W. H. (2003). *The human web: A birds-eye view of world history*. W. W. Norton.

Minkova, D., & Stockwell, R. (2009). *English words: History and structure* (2nd ed.). Cambridge University Press.

Montgomery, S. L. (2013). *Does science need a global language? English and the future of research*. The University of Chicago Press.

Morris, I. (2011). *Why the West rules—For now: The patterns of history, and what they reveal about the future*. Profile Books.

Mufwene, S. S. (2001). *The ecology of language evolution*. Cambridge University Press.

Mühlhäusler, P. (2010). Ecology of languages. In R. B. Kaplan (Ed.), *The Oxford handbook of applied linguistics* (2nd ed., pp. 421–434). Oxford.

Nettle, D., & Romaine, S. (2000). *Vanishing voices: The extinction of the world's languages*. Oxford University Press.

Nolan, P., & Lenski, G. (2015). *Human societies: An introduction to macrosociology* (12th ed.). Oxford University Press.

Northrup, D. (2013). *How English became the global language*. Palgrave Macmillan.

Norton, B. (2000). *Identity and language learning: Gender, ethnicity and educational change*. Pearson Education Limited.

Norton, B., & Gao, Y. (2008). Identity, investment, and Chinese learners of English. *Journal of Asian Pacific Communication, 18*(1), 109–120.

Norton Peirce, B. (1995). Social identity, investment, and language learning. *TESOL Quarterly, 29*(1), 9–31.

Ostler, N. (2011). Language maintenance, shift, and endangerment. In R. Mesthrie (Ed.), *The Cambridge handbook of sociolinguistics* (pp. 315–334). Cambridge University Press.

Park, J. S., & Wee, L. (2012). *Markets of English: Linguistic capital and language policy in a globalizing world*. Routledge.

Piller, I., & Grey, A. (2019). General introduction: Language and globalization—Mapping the field. In I. Piller & A. Grey (Eds.), *Language and globalization: Critical concepts in linguistics* (Vol. 1, pp. 1–37). Routledge.

Pomeranz, K. (2000). *The great divergence: China, Europe, and the making of the modern world economy*. Princeton University Press.

Scholte, J. A. (2005). *Globalization: A critical introduction* (2nd ed.). Palgrave Macmillan.

Schneider, E. W. (2011). Colonization, globalization, and the sociolinguistics of World Englishes. In R. Mesthrie (Ed.), *The Cambridge handbook of sociolinguistics* (pp. 335–353). Cambridge University Press.

Shambaugh, D. (2020). China's long march to global power. In D. Shambaugh (Ed.), *China and the world* (pp. 3–21). Oxford University Press.

Simmons, I. G. (1996). *Changing the face of the earth: Culture, environment, history* (2nd ed.). Blackwell.

Svartvik, J., & Leech, G. (2006). *English: One tongue, many voices*. Palgrave Macmillan.

Wright, S. (2016). *Language policy and language planning: From nationalism to globalisation* (2nd ed.). Palgrave Macmillan.

Xu, J. (2007). 语言规划与语言教育. *Language planning and language education*. Xuelin Press.

Zhang, W. F. (2012). Has Beijing started to bare its teeth? China's tapping of soft power revisited. *Asian Perspective, 36*(4), 615–639.

Zhou, M. (2019). *Language ideology and order in rising China*. Palgrave Macmillan.

Zou, J. & You, R. (2001). 汉语与华人社会. *The Chinese language and Chinese society*. Fudan University Press.

CHAPTER 3

The Language Comprehensive Competitiveness of Chinese: The Objective Perspective

Abstract This chapter analyses media documents, websites, government surveys and reports, statistical compilations and academic works relevant to each component of language comprehensive competitiveness. It shows that geostrategic, population and economic competitiveness most strongly support the macroacquisition of Chinese in objective terms, while policy, cultural, scientific/technological and educational competitiveness offer less support. Script competitiveness is the component of language comprehensive competitiveness which offers the least support for the macroacquisition of Chinese in objective terms because the character-based script presents obstacles to macroacquisition.

Keywords Chinese · Language comprehensive competitiveness · Objective perspective

3.1 INTRODUCTION

Chinese has a particular niche—a set of domains and functions—in the global ecology of languages. This niche means certain resources are available in and through the language, and these in turn demonstrate the association of Chinese with the various forms of power as represented

J. Gil, *The Rise of Chinese as a Global Language*, https://doi.org/10.1007/978-3-030-76171-4_3

in the components of language comprehensive competitiveness. Mapping out this niche gives the objective perspective on the macroacquisition of Chinese.

I do this by presenting the findings of my secondary analysis of sources relevant to each component of language comprehensive competitiveness and making comparisons to English, the current global language. Table 3.1 shows examples of the indicators of each component of language comprehensive competitiveness I looked for. I draw on media reports, websites, government surveys and reports, statistical compilations and academic works to argue that geostrategic, economic and population competitiveness most strongly support the marcoacquisition of Chinese in objective terms, while policy, cultural, scientific/technological and educational competitiveness offer some support, but not as much. Script competitiveness is the component of language comprehensive competitiveness which offers the least support for the macroacquisition of Chinese in objective terms (Table 3.1).

3.2   POLICY COMPETITIVENESS

Various governments have undertaken language planning and enacted language policy which emphasises and promotes the use of Chinese. The variety of Chinese in question here is Mandarin. Mandarin has official status in the PRC, Hong Kong Special Administrative Region (HKSAR), Macau Special Administrative Region (MSAR), Taiwan and Singapore. Across these areas there are three national standard varieties of Mandarin: Putonghua in the PRC, HKSAR and MSAR, Guoyu in Taiwan, and Huayu in Singapore. In all these areas, governments have vigorously promoted the use of the national standard variety so that they are now the main medium of formal and important domains such as administration, education and the mass media (Chen, 2007; Simpson, 2007a, 2007b). This is considerably less official status than English, which is an official or co-official language in over 70 countries spread across Africa, Asia and the Pacific (Crystal, 2006).

Second/foreign language education planning and language policy also emphasises and promotes Chinese, and here too the variety is Mandarin. Many governments and other institutions have implemented or expanded Chinese language education. For example, Chinese became a compulsory subject in Kenyan primary schools from Grade 4 from 2020, and is also compulsory for two years of senior secondary school in Uganda

Table 3.1 Indicators of components of language comprehensive competitiveness

Component	Definition	Example indicators
Policy competitiveness	Emphasis on use of the language and promotion in language planning and language policy of governments and international organisations	• Official language policies • Second/foreign language education policies • International organisations' language policies
Cultural competitiveness	Vitality, prestige and popularity of traditional and contemporary culture associated with the language	• Publications • TV and movies • Internet content • Cultural practices
Economic competitiveness	Economic development and economic power of the country in which the language is spoken	• GDP growth • Size of economy • Imports and exports • Rank as trading partner • Outward Foreign Direct Investment
Population competitiveness	Number of speakers of the language and number of second/additional language learners	• Number of native speakers • Number of second/additional language learners • Distribution of speakers in world
Scientific/technological competitiveness	New developments and advances in science and technology in the country where the language is spoken and utility of the language as a means to access information about such advances and developments	• Inventions • Innovations • Publications
Educational competitiveness	Quality of education, especially higher education, and scholarly research in the country where the language is spoken, and the utility of the language to access education and research	• University rankings • International students

(continued)

Table 3.1   (continued)

Component	Definition	Example indicators
Geostrategic competitiveness	Extent of interests of the country where the language is spoken in the international system, and its influence within the international system	• Number and nature of interactions with countries/regions • Influence on international events and issues

(Adegoke, 2018; Dahir, 2019). In England, 13% of state secondary schools and 46% of independent schools offered Chinese as of 2015 (British Association for Chinese Studies, n.d.). Some schools have made it compulsory, such as the state school Kingsford Community School, where students must study Mandarin as well as French, and the private school Brighton College, where Mandarin instruction begins in preparatory school (G. X. Zhang & L. M. Li, 2010). The UK's Mandarin Excellence Programme, which aims to produce at least 5000 students proficient in Chinese through intensive language study, covers 64 schools (IOE Confucius Institute for Schools, 2017a, 2017b). Saudi Arabia will add Chinese to the curriculum from school to university level to enhance relations with China and achieve the educational goals of its Vision 2030 policy (*Al Arabiya English*, 2019).

Chinese was classified as a foreign language critical to the USA's security interests under the National Flagship Language Initiative, while the College Board introduced the AP Chinese Language and Culture program aimed at promoting and supporting Chinese in schools through provision of guest teachers from China, study trips to China for teachers, teacher training opportunities and assistance with existing or new Mandarin courses (Goh & Lim, 2010; Zhou, 2011). In Australia, Chinese has been recognised as a priority language in foreign language teaching since the mid-1990s, under both the National Asian Languages and Studies in Australian Schools (NALSAS) plan and the National Asian Languages and Studies in Schools Program (NALSSP) (Lo Bianco, 2012; Slaughter, 2011).

While not all of these initiatives have been successful in achieving their goals, they nevertheless demonstrate the growing profile of Chinese in language planning and language policy in second/foreign language education. However, Chinese is not yet on the same level as English in language education policy and planning globally. According to Crystal (2006), English is the priority foreign language in more than 100 countries spread across Europe, Asia, Africa and Latin America. International organisations do not emphasise or promote the use of Chinese to the same degree, as in most cases English is the designated official and/or working language or one of the languages with this function. However, Chinese does have some standing in such organisations, and again the variety under discussion is Mandarin. Chinese is one of the six official languages of the United Nations (Wu, 2010). In January 2021, Chinese was added to the list of official languages of the United Nations World Tourism Organisation (UNWTO) alongside English, Spanish, French, Arabic and Russian (CGTN, 2021). It is also one of six official languages of the International Criminal Court (ICC), in which judgements and decisions are published, although the ICC's working languages are English and French (ICC, 2011). The Shanghai Cooperation Organisation (SCO) has Chinese and Russian as its official languages (Shanghai Cooperation Organisation, 2021). Many other international organisations, such as the International Monetary Fund (IMF), World Bank and World Trade Organisation (WTO), offer interpretation and translation into Mandarin or provide information in Mandarin (IMF, 2019; World Bank, 2021a; WTO, 2021).

Chinese therefore has extensive support in the language planning and language policy of governments in the areas where it spoken natively, a significant role in language planning and language policy in second/foreign language education, and a limited role in the language planning and language policy of international organisations.

3.3 Cultural Competitiveness

Traditional Chinese culture is well known throughout the world. Many aspects of it are popular, such as medicine, architecture, cuisine and martial arts, as evidenced by their presence in many countries.

As for contemporary culture, there is a significant amount of news, publications, television programs, movies and Internet content available in Chinese. For example, over 500 kinds of publication are currently produced outside of China, including daily and weekly newspapers and magazines, many of which also have online editions (Goh & Lim, 2010; Wu, 2010). Several major media outlets, including the BBC and Reuters, have also established Chinese editions online (Goh & Lim, 2010; Wu, 2010). In terms of television, broadcasts from stations in China such as GCTV, Asia Satellite TV, Phoenix Satellite TV Chinese Channel and MTV Chinese Channel are accessible overseas, and many countries have also established their own Chinese language television broadcasts including the USA, Thailand, Japan and Australia (Wu, 2010).

China's box office revenues were among the fastest growing in the world in the early 2000s, and by 2019 China had become the second biggest country in the film industry with US$9.3 billion in revenue. It also produced four of the top twenty grossing feature films of 2019 (China Power, 2019; Lampton, 2008). In early 2019, the director of the National Film Bureau, Wang Xiaohui, expressed the desire for China to match the USA's standing in the film industry by 2035 (China Power, 2019).

Some Chinese movies have had success globally, including *Crouching Tiger, Hidden Dragon*, *Hero* and *House of Flying Daggers*. *Crouching Tiger, Hidden Dragon* was the first foreign language film to take over US$100 million at the American box office, and also won four Academy Awards from ten nominations (Ding & Saunders, 2006).[1] However, Chinese movies generally struggle outside of China. According to analysis by China Power (2019), the top twenty grossing Chinese feature films since 2005 earned less than 1% of their total revenue from overseas. This is in stark contrast to American feature films which earn around 66% of their total revenue overseas.

The presence of Chinese on the Internet has also expanded in recent decades, with over 888 million Chinese speaking Internet users, representing 19.4% of the world's total users, and second only to English. The number of Chinese speaking internet users increased by 2650.4% from 2000 to 2020 (Internet World Statistics, 2020). Chinese can also be used in search engines such as Yahoo, Google and Baidu (Goh & Lim, 2010; Wu, 2010), further adding to the volume of Chinese cultural products and enabling them to be experienced directly from anywhere with an Internet connection.

This is certainly significant, although English remains the main language of the world's books, newspapers, movies, television programmes and popular music (Crystal, 2003). Lampton (2008) argued that contemporary cultural products created elsewhere are far more influential than China's at the time he wrote his book, and this is largely still the case today. Chinese culture, therefore, is well-known, and certain Chinese cultural products have achieved global popularity, but not to the same degree as English language cultural products.

3.4 ECONOMIC COMPETITIVENESS

China's economic development has been spectacular over the past several decades, with annual GDP growth averaging almost 10% from 1978 to 2010. China is now an upper-middle-income country and has been the world's second largest economy since 2010 (Naughton, 2020; World Bank, 2021b). It had a GDP of US$14.3 trillion in 2019, representing two-thirds of the USA's US$21.4 trillion (World Bank, 2021c). Its GDP represented 18.7% of the global total in 2018 in purchasing parity terms, and it accounted for 27.2% of global growth in 2017 (Shambaugh, 2020b).

China is also the world's largest trader, having 12.4% of global trade (totalling US$4.6 trillion) by 2018. It is the largest exporter and the second-largest importer of goods, with 13.45% (over US$2.49 trillion) and 11.37% (US$2.13 trillion) of the world's total respectively. China has also become a major importer of services, with US$470 billion worth of imports in 2017, compared to only US$36 billion in 2000 (China Power, 2020). Furthermore, China is the primary trading partner of 124 countries (Shambaugh, 2020b).

While China's outward foreign direct investment (OFDI) has declined since 2017 due to stricter policies and controls, it remains an important investor. In 2019, its OFDI was US$118 billion (Chen & Findlay, 2020; *South China Morning Post*, 2020). This combined role as an importer, exporter and investor creates a range of employment and development opportunities in other countries, giving China significant economic influence and attraction (Lampton, 2008).

China's growth has of course slowed in recent years due to declining labour force growth and migration of rural labourers to urban areas, as well as the maturation of domestic industries. It also faces a number of economic challenges, chief among them overcoming the middle-income trap so it can reach the level of a fully developed high-income country (Naughton, 2020; World Bank, 2021b). Furthermore, according to the World Bank (2021b), China's per capita income is approximately one-quarter of the per capita income in high-income countries, and around 373 million people are still living below the upper-middle-income poverty line of US$5.50 a day.

It is by no means guaranteed that China will be able to overcome these challenges. However, it will likely remain very influential economically for several decades, with a projected GDP of US$16.7 trillion to US$19.5 trillion by 2025, and US$30.16 trillion to US$46.74 trillion in 2040 (Naughton, 2020; Shambaugh, 2020b).

3.5   Population Competitiveness

Chinese, in all its varieties, has the largest number of native speakers of any language in the world, totalling more than one billion. This surpasses the 400 million native speakers of English (Crystal, 2006). Mandarin makes up a significant proportion of the total number of native speakers. In the PRC, approximately 70% of the population speaks Mandarin as their native language (Lyovin et al., 2017). Its standard variety, Putonghua, has spread considerably in recent decades. According to the Ministry of Education, 73% of the population were able to speak Putonghua by 2015, up from 53% in 2000 (Xinhua, 2017).

Similar trends can be found with the national standard varieties of Mandarin used elsewhere. In Singapore, for example, at the time of the 2000 census, 45.1% of the Chinese resident population aged five years and over spoke Huayu in the home. This increased to 47.7% in 2010. The use of other varieties of Chinese in the home decreased over the same period, from 30.7% in 2000 to 19.2% in 2010 (Statistics Singapore, 2011). Taiwan too has seen an increase in speakers of Guoyu. Simpson (2007a) estimated that up to 95% of the population can speak and understand Guoyu to varying degrees. These standard varieties of Mandarin function as intranational lingua francas for speakers of different varieties of Chinese in these areas and in some cases also for non-Chinese ethnic groups living within these areas (D. C. S. Li, 2006).

Some scholars have argued that the large numbers of speakers of Chinese "are in the main ethnically and culturally homogenous" and their "worldwide distribution is limited" (McArthur, 2002, p. 414) to the geographical areas discussed above. This seemingly contrasts with the distribution of native speakers of English, which as Crystal (2006) explains, covers the USA, Canada, Britain, Ireland, Australia, New Zealand, South Africa and a few other regions such as the Caribbean. However, the overseas Chinese population should also be considered when discussing population competitiveness. There are over 45 million ethnic Chinese living outside of mainland China, Taiwan, Hong Kong and Macau, and this could increase to over 59 million by 2040. This large population is distributed across some 130 countries (P. S. Li & E. X. Li, 2013). Until recently, Min, Yue and Kejia were the most commonly used varieties within the Chinese diaspora, but Mandarin has become increasingly prominent as a result of China's economic development. Related to this, Putonghua is also arguably becoming the lingua franca of the diaspora (Li, 2016).

The number of people learning a language is another aspect of its population competitiveness. de Swaan (2001) explains that learner numbers are important because learners are likely to come from a variety of language backgrounds, so learning a language which has a lot of learners can facilitate communication with speakers of many other languages. While such figures can never be exact, a commonly cited estimate is that there are 100 million people learning Chinese (*China Daily*, 2017). Mandarin is the variety of Chinese most often learned. Learners come from many different countries and therefore language backgrounds. This means that learning Chinese also potentially confers the additional advantage of being able to converse with speakers of other languages through Mandarin.

While this is a large number of learners, it should be noted there are currently far more Chinese learning English than there are English speakers learning Chinese. Estimates of learners of English in China vary from 200 to over 400 million (Bolton, 2008; Crystal, 2008; Zhao & Campbell, 1995). Altogether, there are estimated to be as many as 1.5 billion people learning English in the world (ICEF Monitor, 2019). There are also more speakers of other languages learning English than Chinese (Bruthiaux, 2002; McArthur, 2005). This means English is still the language that allows communication with the greatest number of people.

3.6   Script Competitiveness

Gnanadesikan (2009) describes writing as "one of the most important human inventions of all time" (p. 2). Writing allows information to be recorded and stored in greater quantities and levels of detail than the human memory can manage, and enables information to be communicated over time and across space. According to some estimates, only 200 to 300 of the world's languages currently have a written script (Montgomery, 2013).

Chinese is one of these languages, and has a logographic script. This means that each unit of the script, or character, represents a morpheme as well as a syllable. In many cases, a single morpheme and syllable also constitute a word (Lyovin et al., 2017).[2] There are, however, some exceptions, including disyllabic words like 葡萄 *pútao* "grape", and 琵琶 *pípá*, a Chinese musical instrument, as well as some transliterated Chinese expressions in translated Buddhist texts. Characters are composed of lines and dots, known as strokes, written with a single movement of a pen. There are 24 strokes altogether, and characters can range from a single stroke to tens of strokes. All characters are written as though they were surrounded by a square boundary (Gao, 2000; Taylor & Taylor, 2014).

There are three main types of characters: pictographs, loan graphs and phonographs. Pictographs are direct representations of objects. Examples include 山 *shān* "mountain", 田 *tián* "field" and 口 *kǒu* "mouth". Loan graphs are characters that are used to represent two or more different words with the same pronunciation. Both "foot" and "sufficient" are pronounced *zú*, for instance, and are written with the same character, 足. Loan graphs came about because at some point in history the character used to write one word was used to write another with the same pronunciation but different meaning (Kane, 2006).

Over 80% of characters are phonographs, which means they are composed of two parts, a phonetic determinative which provides some information about how the character is pronounced, and a semantic component called a radical, which gives information about the character's meaning (Kane, 2006). The character 青 is pronounced *qīng*, and by itself means "green". When it is used as a phonetic determinative, different radicals can be added to change its meaning while retaining the same pronunciation (except for changes in tone in some cases). For example, adding the radical 日 (*rì* = sun) gives 晴 *qíng*, meaning "sunny", adding the radical 鱼 (*yú* = fish) gives 鲭 *qīng*, meaning "mackerel" and adding the radical 讠 (*yán* = words) gives 请 *qǐng*, meaning "please". There are around 200 radicals and several thousand phonetic determinatives which combine in this way, although not every radical can be combined with every phonetic determinative (Gao, 2000; Xing, 2006).

The helpfulness of the phonetic determinatives is limited in a number of ways. To begin with, it is not always clear which part of a character is the phonetic determinative and which part is the semantic component, as both can appear in any position, including on the left, right, top, bottom, inside or outside of a character, and some parts can function as both phonetic determinatives and semantic components (Taylor & Taylor, 2014). Phonetic determinatives do not indicate tone at all, and often give only part of a character's pronunciation, such as the final sound. Sound changes in the language over time also mean around a third of phonetic determinatives do not reflect current pronunciation, and even when they do, the high number of homophones in Chinese means the same phonetic determinative is used in many different words (Gnanadesikan, 2009; Moser, 2016). Taylor and Taylor (2014) also point out that some knowledge of characters is required to know the sound of the phonetic determinative, and as such they are not useful for complete beginner learners. The Chinese writing system cannot therefore be described as phonetic in any meaningful sense, making Chinese virtually unique among the world's languages (Chen, 1999).

This presents constraints to the macroacquisition of Chinese. To begin with, many learners find characters difficult and time-consuming to learn. Kane (2006) claimed that learners of Chinese could realistically learn only around 30 characters a week. This means considerable time and effort are required to learn the 5000 to 7000 characters a well-educated Chinese person could be expected to know, and to enable learners to read contemporary authentic materials (Taylor & Taylor, 2014). In comparison, learners can usually learn a complete alphabetic or syllabic written script and begin to use it to read and write in a much shorter time (Dobrovolsky, 2011).

In addition, there are two versions of the script, the simplified characters, or 简体字 *jiǎntǐzì*, used in the PRC, and the complex characters, or 繁体字 *fántǐzì*, used in Taiwan.[3] This potentially causes confusion for language learners and impedes communication among others, lessening the utility of Chinese characters as a vehicle of communication globally (Goh & Lim, 2010; Premaratne, 2012). Thirdly, there are some difficulties with the digitisation of characters. There are a number of very different input systems which are often incompatible, and as a result, there can be significant problems with the electronic transmission of information written in characters (Premaratne, 2012; Zhao, 2010). Zhao (2010) holds that this is a major dilemma because, as computers are so important in today's world, any language that cannot be effectively digitised will be largely confined to its own physical territory and lack influence elsewhere. Therefore, while Chinese has a written script, its use in certain domains and its acquisition can be problematic.[4]

3.7   SCIENTIFIC/TECHNOLOGICAL COMPETITIVENESS

Since the 2000s, China has endeavoured to enhance its standing as a scientific and technological power. In 2006, then-President Hu Jintao announced the Medium and Long Term Plan for Science and Technology Development to make China an innovator in these fields, and made a series of recommendations to achieve this. These included increasing research and development spending to 2.5% of GDP by 2020; establishing more foreign research and development facilities in China; establishing more Chinese research and development facilities overseas; and increasing the links between universities, businesses and government. More recently, current President Xi Jinping launched the Made in China 2025 initiative aimed at increasing quality manufacturing through innovation. The 13th Five Year Plan (2016–2020) also incorporated goals for innovation in science and technology, scholarly citations, patents and scientific literacy among the country's population. These are intended to make China a world class innovator by 2050 (Han & Appelbaum, 2018; Lampton, 2008).

Data from the US National Science Board Science and Engineering Indicators 2020 demonstrate that China's science and technology capabilities are growing. For example, over 1.7 million science and engineering first university degrees were awarded in China in 2016 (compared to just over 768,000 in the USA), of which 70% were in engineering. China also had the greatest increase in number of first degrees of countries covered in the report. As for doctoral degrees, China awarded almost 35,000 in science and engineering in 2015, behind the USA which awarded close to 40,000 in 2016. However, China overtook the USA as the producer of the largest number of doctoral degrees in natural sciences and engineering in 2007 and has retained this potion (National Science Board, 2020).

China had the second-largest gross domestic expenditure on R&D in 2017 (US$496 billion in PPP dollars), behind the USA (US$549 billion in PPP dollars) but ahead of the European Union (US$430.1 billion in PPP dollars). China made up 23% of global R&D in 2017, a close second to the USA with 25%. China was also responsible for 32% of global growth in R&D expenditure from 2000 to 2017, with the USA second on 20% (National Science Board, 2020). China has prioritised aerospace and aviation equipment, artificial intelligence, robotics, nanotechnology, biotechnology, medical devices, electric vehicles, advanced rail equipment, IT, new materials, cloud computing and semi-conductors. If its R&D

spending continues at current levels or increases, China will likely be one of the leaders in these fields (Shambaugh, 2020b).

China's output of peer-reviewed science and engineering publications made up 21% of the world's total in 2018, a drastic increase from just 5% in 2000. This places China third behind the European Union (27%) and the USA (17%). Engineering was a particular strength of China's, as it produced more articles than both the European Union and the USA. Its top 1% of cited articles index (a country's share of top cited articles compared to its total publication output) increased from 0.4 to 1.1 between 2000 and 2016, placing it third behind the USA and European Union (National Science Board, 2020). Some of these publications would undoubtedly be in English, especially those published in international journals. As Montgomery (2013) points out, many Chinese scholars in these fields want to publish in English to ensure their work is accessible to a wide audience. Han and Appelbaum (2018) similarly point out that many Chinese universities offer their staff incentives to publish in English.

However, the presence of Chinese in science research should not be underestimated. According to Xie and Freeman (2018), scientific publication in Chinese actually increased from 2000 to 2016 along with an increase of such publications in English. This contrasts with the pattern often observed in other countries. In early 2020, the Ministry of Education and the Ministry of Science and Technology announced changes to how researchers would be evaluated. These included a requirement that a minimum of one-third of publications used to evaluate them must be in domestic journals. A list of priority journals contains almost half which publish in Chinese (MoChridhe, 2020).

China also had 49% of worldwide patent families granted in 2018, more than any other country (National Science Board, 2020). For a long time, China had a reputation as an innovator in the sense of putting existing components, technologies, or concepts together in new ways which better suit customers domestically and internationally, and being adept at making improvements to a product's manufacturing process, performance and time to market (Lampton, 2008). Whether this changes with China's R&D spending remains to be seen.

Several problems constrain China's ambitions of becoming a world leader in science and technology. These include academic fraud, mismanagement and corruption of research talent and funding, excessive government intervention into research and universities and an emphasis on quantity of research outputs over quality (Han & Appelbaum, 2018).

Science and technology are therefore areas in which China is making significant progress but is not yet a global leader.

3.8   EDUCATIONAL COMPETITIVENESS

As with science and technology, China has devoted significant effort and resources to improving its education system in recent years. Most of this has focused on higher education, with the aim to develop internationally competitive and recognised universities. The 211 Project, initiated in 1993, for example, aimed to identify 100 universities and a range of disciples which could achieve world standing in the twenty-first century through preferential funding and development arrangements. Similarly, the 985 Project, launched in 1998, aimed to develop approximately 40 of China's elite universities into world-class universities with strong international reputations through the provision of substantial extra funding (Y. Li et al., 2008; Mohrman, 2008).

There has certainly been some progress in the world rankings of China's universities. According to the Shanghai Jiao Tong University Academic Ranking of World Universities, China has 168 universities in the world top 1000 universities, 49 in the top 500, 16 in the top 200 and six in the top 100 (Academic Ranking of World Universities, 2020). This is an increase on previous years, although American, British and European institutions still make up most of the top-placed universities.

According to the Institute of International Education's Project Atlas data, China is the third-largest destination for international students in the world after the USA and the UK (Institute of International Education, 2019). In 2018, there were 492,185 international students from 196 countries and regions in China, representing an increase of 0.62% from 2017. Of these students, 258,122 were degree students while 234,063 were non-degree students. 85,062 international students were enrolled in postgraduate level study, including 59,444 master students and 25,618 PhD students. Most of these students come from other Asian countries, with South Korea, Thailand and Pakistan the top three source countries (Ministry of Education of the People's Republic of China, 2019). It should be noted that many Chinese universities offer courses through English as the medium of instruction, especially in science and technology, and this may account for some of the growth in international student numbers (Gil & Adamson, 2011; Montgomery, 2013).

However, the USA remains the leading destination for international students, with over 1.095 million international students in the 2018 to 2019 academic year and over 1.075 million in 2019 to 2020 academic year. China was the largest source country, supplying 35% of these students (Institute of International Education, 2020). China was also the largest source country of international students in the UK, Australia, New Zealand, Japan and Germany, the second-largest source country of international students in Canada and Russia, the third-largest source country for international students in the Netherlands, France and Sweden and the fourth largest source country of international students in Finland and Norway (Institute of International Education, 2019). This suggests other countries' universities are still more appealing than China's. China's education and research are therefore making progress, although remain some distance behind the current world leaders.

3.9 Geostrategic Competitiveness

China has interests in all areas of the world. Nathan and Scobell (2012) conceptualise China's interests as four rings that stretch from China to the rest of the world. The first ring encompasses China's own territory and territories it claims as its own, such as islands in the East China Sea and South China Sea. China's primary interests in this ring are maintaining domestic political stability and minimising foreign influence. The second ring covers the twenty countries which directly border China. Here China's interests are protecting itself from external threats as well as countering the military, economic and diplomatic influence of the USA on these countries.

The overlapping regional systems of Northeast Asia (Russia, North and South Korea, Japan, China and the USA), Oceania (Australia, New Zealand, Papua New Guinea, Fiji, the Pacific microstates, China and the USA), continental Southeast Asia (Vietnam, Cambodia, Laos, Thailand, Burma, China and the USA), maritime Southeast Asia (Vietnam, Malaysia, Singapore, Indonesia, Brunei, the Philippines, China and the USA), South Asia (Burma, Bangladesh, India, Nepal, Bhutan, Pakistan, Sri Lanka, the Maldives, Russia, China and the USA) and Central Asia (Russia, Kazakhstan, Kyrgyzstan, Tajikistan, Uzbekistan, Turkmenistan, Afghanistan China and the USA) make up the third ring. China's interests in this ring vary somewhat across the different regional systems, but centre on manging interactions with others to ensure China's security and gaining acceptance of its rise. Finally, the fourth ring consists of Eastern and Western Europe, the Middle East and North and South America. China's interests in this ring are accessing energy resources, markets, investment opportunities and commodities and seeking diplomatic support for its policies and positions in global politics.

In addition to these wide-ranging interests, China's input and cooperation are also necessary to solve global issues such as climate change. All countries and international organisations must therefore pay attention to China to some degree (Nathan & Scobell, 2012). However, China is still not able to project its power and influence events globally to the same extent as the USA. According to Shambaugh (2020a), China has a significant and growing global presence but its actual influence over the behaviour of other actors and the outcome of events lags behind.

3.10   Conclusion

In this chapter, I examined the macroacquisition of Chinese from the objective perspective. Based on the resources available in and through Chinese, the three components of geostrategic, economic and population competitiveness offer the strongest support for macroacquisition, followed by policy, cultural, scientific/technological and educational competitiveness. Script competitiveness offers the least support for macroacquistion.

The objective state of Chinese in the global ecology of languages is however only part of the picture. It is also necessary to look at how Chinese is perceived by those who seek to acquire it as a second/additional language. This is the subject of the next chapter, where I explore the subjective perspective on the macroacquisition of Chinese.

Notes

1. This film was jointly funded by China, Hong Kong, Taiwan and the USA.
2. Lyovin et al. (2017) suggests the term morphemographic as a more accurate description of the Chinese writing system and Daniels (1990) suggests logosyllabographic. As neither of these terms have been widely adopted, I have not used them here. DeFrancis (1989) has also argued that the Chinese writing system can be regarded as a syllabary, albeit a very complex one. The details of this argument are beyond the scope of this chapter.
3. In addition, two major phonetic transcription systems are also currently in wide use, namely 汉语拼音 *hànyǔ pīnyīn*, comprising symbols derived

from the Roman alphabet and used in the PRC, and 注音符号 *zhùyīnfúhào*, comprising symbols derived from Chinese characters, and used in Taiwan (Kane, 2006).
4. I provide a fuller discussion of the character based script and its impact on the future of Chinese as a global language in Chapter 6.

REFERENCES

Academic Ranking of World Universities. (2020). *Academic ranking of world universities 2020: China*. Retrieved 10 December, 2020, from http://www.shanghairanking.com/World-University-Rankings-2020/China.html
Adegoke, Y. (2018, December 23). Uganda is adding compulsory Chinese lessons to its high school curriculum. *Quartz Africa*. Retrieved 29 January, 2019, from https://qz.com/africa/1505985/uganda-schools-to-teach-chinese-lessons/
Al Arabiya English. (2019). Saudi Arabia to include Chinese language in educational curriculum. Retrieved 27 February, 2019, from https://eng lish.alarabiya.net/en/News/gulf/2019/02/22/Saudi-Arabia-to-include-Chi nese-language-in-educational-curriculum.html
Bolton, K. (2008). English in Asia, Asian Englishes, and the issue of proficiency. *English Today, 24*(2), 3–12.
British Association for Chinese Studies. (n.d.). *Chinese in UK schools*. Retrieved 8 December, 2020, from http://bacsuk.org.uk/chinese-in-uk-schools
Bruthiaux, P. (2002). Predicting challenges to English as a global language in the 21st century. *Language Problems & Language Planning, 26*(2), 12–157.
CGTN. (2021). Chinese becomes an official language of the UNWTO. Retrieved 25 February, 2021, from https://news.cgtn.com/news/2021-02-21/Chinese-becomes-an-official-language-of-the-UNWTO-Y3u391Cr9C/index.html
Chen, C., & Findlay, C. (2020, June 10). China's foreign direct investment flows: The role of foreign spending in China's pandemic rebound. *Asia & the Pacific Policy Society Policy Forum*. Retrieved 10 December, 2020, from https://www.policyforum.net/chinas-foreign-direct-investment-flows/
Chen, P. (1999). *Modern Chinese: History and sociolinguistics*. Cambridge: Cambridge University Press.
Chen, P. (2007). China. In A. Simpson (Ed.), *Language and national identity in Asia* (pp. 141–167). Oxford University Press.
China Daily. (2017). *Mandarin is now rapidly becoming a global language*. Retrieved 15 February, 2019, from http://www.chinadaily.com.cn/opinion/2017-10/13/content_33190150.htm
China Power. (2019). *Do Chinese films hold global appeal?* Retrieved 10 December, 2020, from https://chinapower.csis.org/chinese-films/

China Power. (2020). *Is China the world's top trader?* Retrieved 10 December, 2020, from https://chinapower.csis.org/trade-partner/

Crystal, D. (2003). *English as a global language* (2nd ed.). Cambridge University Press.

Crystal, D. (2006). English worldwide. In R. Hogg & D. Denison (Eds.), *A history of the English language* (pp. 420–439). Cambridge University Press.

Crystal, D. (2008). Two thousand million? *English Today, 24*(1), 3–6

Dahir, A. L. (2019, January 8). Kenya will start teaching Chinese to elementary school students from 2020. *Quartz Africa.* Retrieved 29 January, 2019, from https://qz.com/africa/1517681/kenya-to-teach-mandarin-chinese-in-primary-classrooms/

Daniels, P. T. (1990). Fundamentals of grammatology. *Journal of the American Oriental Society, 110*(4), 727–731.

DeFrancis, J. (1989). *Visible speech: The diverse oneness of writing systems.* University of Hawaii Press.

de Swaan, A. (2001). *Words of the world: The global language system.* Polity Press.

Ding, S., & Saunders, R. A. (2006). Talking up China: An analysis of China's rising cultural power and global promotion of the Chinese language. *East Asia, 23*(2), 3–33.

Dobrovolsky, M. (2011). Writing and language. In W. O'Grady, J. Archibald & F. Katamba (Eds.), *Contemporary linguistics: An introduction* (2nd ed.) (pp. 523–546). Pearson Education Limited.

Gao, M. C. F. (2000). *Mandarin Chinese: An introduction.* Oxford University Press.

Gil, J., & Adamson, B. (2011). The English language in mainland China: A sociolinguistic profile. In A. Feng (Ed.), *English language education across greater China* (pp. 23-45). Multilingual Matters.

Gnanadesikan, A. E. (2009). *The writing revolution: Cuneiform to the Internet.* Wiley-Blackwell.

Goh, Y. S., & Lim, S. L. (2010). Global mandarin. In V. Vaish (Ed.), *Globalization of language and culture in Asia: The impact of globalization processes on language* (pp. 14–33). Continuum.

Han, X., & Appelbaum, R. P. (2018). China's science, technology, engineering, and mathematics (STEM) research environment: A snapshot. *PLoS ONE, 13*(4). https://doi.org/10.1371/journal.pone.0195347

International Criminal Court (ICC). (2011). *Rome Statue of the International Criminal Court.* Retrieved 7 January, 2021, from http://www.icc-cpi.int/NR/rdonlyres/ADD16852-AEE9-4757-ABE7-9CDC7CF02886/283503/RomeStatutEngl.pdf

ICEF Monitor. (2019). *The world's changing language landscape.* Retrieved 16 December, 2020, from https://monitor.icef.com/2019/10/the-worlds-changing-language-landscape/

Institute of International Education. (2019). *Project Atlas 2019 release: A quick look at global mobility trends.* Retrieved 26 December, 2020, from file:///C:/Users/61421/Downloads/Project%20Atlas%202019%20graphics.pdf

Institute of International Education. (2020). *Enrollment trends.* Retrieved 26 December, 2020, from https://opendoorsdata.org/data/international-stu dents/enrollment-trends/

International Monetary Fund (IMF). (2019). *International Monetary Fund.* Retrieved 7 January, 2021, from https://www.imf.org/external/index.htm

Internet World Statistics. (2020). *Internet world users by language: Top 10 languages.* Retrieved 8 December, 2020, from https://www.internetworldst ats.com/stats7.htm

IOE Confucius Institute for Schools. (2017a). *Mandarin excellence programme.* Retrieved 15 February, 2019, from https://ci.ioe.ac.uk/mandarin-excellence-programme/

IOE Confucius Institute for Schools. (2017b). *Participating schools.* Retrieved 15 February, 2019, from https://ci.ioe.ac.uk/mandarin-excellence-programme/mep-schools/

Kane, D. (2006). *The Chinese language: Its history and current usage.* Tuttle.

Lampton, D. M. (2008). *The three faces of Chinese power: Might, money and minds.* University of California Press.

Li, D. C. S. (2006). Chinese as a lingua franca in greater China. *Annual Review of Applied Linguistics, 26,* 149–176.

Li, W. (2016). Transnational connections and multilingual realities: The Chinese diasporic experience in a global context. In W. Li (Ed.), *Multilingualism in the Chinese diaspora worldwide: Transnational connections and local social realities* (pp. 1–12). Routledge.

Li, P. S. & Li, E. X. (2013). The overseas Chinese population. In C. B. Tan (Ed.), *Routledge handbook of the Chinese diaspora* (pp. 15–28). Routledge.

Li, Y., Whalley, J., Zhang, S., & Zhao, X. (2008). The higher educational trans- formation of China and its global implications. *NBER Working Paper No. 13849.* Retrieved 7 January, 2021, from http://www.nber.org/papers/w13 849.pdf?new_window=1.

Lo Bianco, J. (2012). Afterword: Tempted by targets, tempered by results. *Australian Review of Applied Linguistics, 35*(3), 359–361.

Lyovin, A. V., Kessler, B., Leben, W. R. (2017). *An introduction to the languages of the world* (2nd ed.). Oxford University Press.

McArthur, T. (2002). *The Oxford guide to world English.* Oxford University Press.

McArthur, T. (2005). Chinese, English, Spanish – And the rest. *English Today, 21*(3), 55–61.

Ministry of Education of the People's Republic of China. (2019). *Statis- tical report on international students in China for 2018.* Retrieved 10

December, 2020, from http://en.moe.gov.cn/documents/reports/201904/
t20190418_378692.html
MoChridhe, R. (2020, November 4). The hidden language policy of China's
research evaluation reform. *Contemporary China Centre Blog*. Retrieved 16
December, 2020, from http://blog.westminster.ac.uk/contemporarychina/
the-hidden-language-policy-of-chinas-research-evaluation-reform/
Mohrman, K. (2008). The emerging global model with Chinese characteristics.
Higher Education Policy, 21, 29–48.
Montgomery, S. L. (2013). *Does science need a global language?: English and the
future of research*. The University of Chicago Press.
Moser, D. (2016). *A billion voices: China's search for a common language*.
Penguin Books.
Nathan, A. J. & Scobell, A. (2012). *China's search for security*. Columbia
University Press.
National Science Board. (2020). *2020 National Science Board
Science & Engineering Indicators: The state of U.S. Science
& Engineering*. Retrieved 10 December, 2020, from
file:///C:/Users/gil0001/AppData/Local/Downloads/nsb20201%20(1).pdf
Naughton, B. (2020). China's global economic interactions. In D. Shambaugh
(Ed.), *China and the world* (pp. 113–136). Oxford University Press.
Premaratne, D. D. (2012). Reforming Chinese characters in the PRC and
Japan: New directions in the twenty-first century. *Current Issues in Language
Planning, 13*(4), 305–319.
Shambaugh, D. (2020a). China's long march to global power. In D. Shambaugh
(Ed.), *China and the world* (pp. 3–21). Oxford University Press.
Shambaugh, D. (2020b). China and the world: Future challenges. In D.
Shambaugh (Ed.), *China and the world* (pp. 343–367). Oxford University
Press.
Shanghai Cooperation Organisation. (2021). *The Shanghai Cooperation Organi-
sation*. Retrieved 27 May, 2021, from http://eng.sectsco.org/about_sco/.
Simpson, A. (2007a). Taiwan. In A. Simpson (Ed.), *Language and national
identity in Asia* (pp. 235–259). Oxford University Press.
Simpson, A. (2007b). Singapore. In A. Simpson (Ed.), *Language and national
identity in Asia* (pp. 374–390). Oxford University Press.
Slaughter, Y. (2011). Bringing Asia to the home front: The Australian experi-
ence of Asian language education through national policy. In C. Norrby & J.
Hajek (Eds.), *Uniformity and diversity in language policy: Global perspectives*
(pp. 157–173). Multilingual Matters.
South China Morning Post. (2020). China's 2019 foreign direct investment grew
most in two years, but outbound investment fell 6 per cent. Retrieved 10
December, 2020, from https://www.scmp.com/economy/china-economy/
article/3046958/chinas-2019-foreign-direct-investment-58-cent-outbound

Statistic Singapore. (2011). *Census of population 2010 statistical release 1: Demographic characteristics, education, language and religion.* Retrieved 8 December, 2020, from https://www.singstat.gov.sg/-/media/files/publicati ons/cop2010/census_2010_release1/cop2010sr1.pdf

Taylor, I. & Taylor, M. M. (2014). *Writing and literacy in Chinese, Korean and Japanese* (Revised ed.). John Benjamins.

World Bank. (2021a). *Language resources.* Retrieved 7 January, 2021, from https://www.worldbank.org/en/language-resources#:~:text=While%20the% 20working%20language%20of,is%20available%20in%20other%20languages

World Bank. (2021b). *The World Bank in China: Overview.* Retrieved 7 January, 2020, from https://www.worldbank.org/en/country/china/overview

World Bank. (2021c). *GDP (current US$).* Retrieved 7 January, 2021, from https://data.worldbank.org/indicator/NY.GDP.MKTP.CD

World Trade Organization (WTO). (2021). *Websites with information on the WTO in non-WTO languages.* Retrieved 7 January, 2021, from https://www. wto.org/english/res_e/links_e/external_links_e.htm

Wu, Y. (2010). 汉语国际传播：新加坡视角视角 *The international promotion of Chinese: A Singaporean perspective.* Commercial Press.

Xie, Q. & Freeman, R. B. (2018). Bigger than you thought: China's contribution to scientific publications. *NBER Working Paper Series Working Paper 24829.* Retrieved 17 December, 2020, from https://www.nber.org/system/files/wor king_papers/w24829/w24829.pdf

Xing, J. Z. (2006). *Teaching and learning Chinese as a foreign language: A pedagogical grammar.* Hong Kong University Press.

Xinhua. (2017). 我国普通话普及率约达 73% (*73% of China's population speak Putonghua*). Retrieved 8 December, 2020, from http://www.xinhuanet. com/politics/2017-09/08/c_1121633180.htm

Zhang, G. X., & Li, L. M. (2010). Chinese language teaching in the UK: Present and future. *Language Learning Journal, 38*(1), 87–97.

Zhao, S. (2010). Flows of technology: Mandarin in cyberspace. In V. Vaish (Ed.), *Globalization of language and culture in Asia: The impact of globalization processes on language* (pp. 139–160). Continuum.

Zhao, Y., & Campbell, K. P. (1995). English in China. *World Englishes, 14*(3), 377–90.

Zhou, M. (2011). Globalization and language order: Teaching Chinese as a foreign language in the United States. In L. Tsung & K. Cruickshank (Eds.), *Teaching and learning Chinese in global contexts: Multimodality and literacy in the new media age* (pp. 131–149). Continuum.

The Language Comprehensive Competitiveness of Chinese: The Subjective Perspective

Abstract This chapter presents the findings of a survey of Chinese language learners, interviews with Chinese language learners, and interviews with Chinese language teachers and Chinese scholars. It argues that geostrategic competitiveness, population competitiveness and economic competitiveness most strongly support the macroacquisition of Chinese in subjective terms. Cultural competitiveness, policy competitiveness and educational competitiveness also offer some support but not as much as these components, and script competitiveness less so. Scientific/technological competitiveness offers the least support for the macroacquisition of Chinese in subjective terms.

Keywords Chinese · Language comprehensive competitiveness · Subjective perspective

4.1 INTRODUCTION

The subjective perspective on the language comprehensive competitiveness of Chinese covers the psychological aspect of its place in the global ecology of languages. It refers to how people perceive or view

Chinese, specifically their perceptions, ideas and beliefs about the associ-ation of Chinese with forms of power and resources represented in the components of language comprehensive competitiveness. Such percep-tions are important because they influence people's decisions about which language(s) to acquire and use (Hornberger & Hult, 2008).

In this chapter I present the findings of my survey of and interviews with Chinese language learners, and interviews with Chinese language teachers and scholars. These indicate that geostrategic competitiveness, population competitiveness and economic competitiveness most strongly support the macroacquisition of Chinese in subjective terms. Cultural competitiveness, policy competitiveness and educational competitiveness also offer some support but not as much as those three components, and script competitiveness even less so. Scientific/technological compet-itiveness offers the least support for the macroacquisition of Chinese in subjective terms.

4.2   CHINESE LANGUAGE LEARNER PARTICIPANTS

Chinese language learners are in the best position to provide data about the subjective aspect of the language comprehensive competitiveness of Chinese because they have made the decision to acquire the language and are able to give reasons for doing so. I contacted learners with the assistance of Chinese language teachers at the universities at which they were enrolled. I obtained Chinese language teachers' email addresses from publicly available university websites then emailed them to request their assistance in contacting and recruiting learners. I provided them with a Letter of Introduction and Information Sheet which explained the purpose of the study and how it would be conducted, as well as the learner questionnaire, and asked them to distribute these to learners in their university through, for example, placing these documents on a notice board or a course website. Learners who wished to participate in the study then completed the questionnaire and returned it to me directly or through their teachers.

A total of 75 Chinese language learners from universities in Australia and China agreed to complete a questionnaire regarding their reasons for learning Chinese and their experiences learning Chinese. Learners were asked to rate, on a scale of 0–10, how important each component of language comprehensive competitiveness was for their decision to learn Chinese and provide a brief explanation of their choice.[1] They were also asked to indicate their willingness to participate in a follow-up email interview, the purpose of which was to gain further details regarding their reasons for learning Chinese.[2] Nine learners chose to do so.

Of the 75 Chinese language learners, 56 were in the 18–24 years age group, 14 were in the 25–34 years age group, one was in the 35–40 years age group and two were in the above 40 years age group. 32 were male and 43 female. A total of 16 different first languages were spoken by participants, with English being the most common (37 participants). With regard to the amount of time participants had been studying Chinese, 45 reported having studied for less than one year, 21 for 1–2 years, seven for 2–3 years, two for 3–4 years and none for more than four years. The vast majority of participants (61) commenced Chinese language study at university, while six commenced their studies of the language in secondary school, one in primary school and seven in other contexts such as language courses after graduation or through their work. 54 participants were taking first year Chinese, 12 second year Chinese, four third year Chinese, one fourth year Chinese and four were taking other kinds of courses such as foundation level studies when the questionnaire was conducted. Almost equal numbers of participants were studying in Australia (37 participants) and China (38 participants). Participants' self-ratings for their current level of proficiency in speaking, listening, reading and writing varied, but most rated themselves limited, fair or good.[3]

Participants are identified by number and country of study only. The abbreviation CLL9 Australia, for example, indicates the comment was made by Chinese Language Learner 9, country of study Australia, while the abbreviation CLL34 China refers to Chinese Language Learner 34, country of study China.

I calculated the average rating of each component of language comprehensive competitiveness from the questionnaires. This information is presented in Table 4.1. I also selected indicative example explanations to demonstrate learners' rationale for their choices, and these are presented throughout the chapter.

4.3   Chinese Language Teacher and Chinese Scholar Participants

Chinese language teachers are also able to provide data about the subjective aspect of the language comprehensive competitiveness of Chinese

Table 4.1 Average rating of each component of language comprehensive competitiveness from learner questionnaire

Component of language comprehensive competitiveness	Average rating
Policy competitiveness	5.29
Cultural competitiveness	6.44
Economic competitiveness	7.21
Population competitiveness	7.32
Script competitiveness	5.08
Scientific/technological competitiveness	4.95
Educational competitiveness	5.25
Geostrategic competitiveness	7.55

because of their academic expertise in Chinese language learning and teaching, and because they are familiar with the reasons why their learners opted to study Chinese. I obtained a list of Chinese language teachers from the websites of university Chinese language departments in Australia and China where potential participants' contact details were publicly available. I emailed these Chinese language teachers a Letter of Introduction and Information Sheet explaining the purpose of the study and how it would be conducted.

A total of 30 Chinese language teachers agreed to participate and completed interviews either via email or in person. Of these, 18 were working at Australian universities and 12 were working at Chinese universities. Chinese language teacher participants were asked to select which component of language comprehensive competitiveness they considered the most important and least important to learners' decision to learn Chinese, and to answer some questions about their experiences teaching Chinese.[4] Here I focus on their selection of the most and least important component of language comprehensive competitiveness to learners' decision to learn Chinese. These results are summarised in Table 4.2. Some teachers provided explanations for their choices and I present these in the relevant sections of this chapter.

I also conducted in-person interviews with three Chinese scholars at a research institute in China. These scholars had expertise in Chinese language, linguistics or applied linguistics, and as such were able to discuss their views on the reasons behind the current interest in Chinese language learning. Like teachers, they were asked to select which component of language comprehensive competitiveness they believed was the most important and least important to learners' decision to learn Chinese, and

Table 4.2 Selection of most and least important component of language comprehensive competitiveness from teacher interviews

Component of language comprehensive competitiveness	Times selected as most important	Times selected as least important
Policy competitiveness	1	0
Cultural competitiveness	2	1
Economic competitiveness	18	0
Population competitiveness	0	0
Script competitiveness	0	17
Scientific/technological competitiveness	0	4
Educational competitiveness	0	7
Geostrategic competitiveness	9	1

answer some questions about Chinese language learning and teaching.[5] For the purposes of this chapter, I concentrate on their responses to the most and least important component of language comprehensive competitiveness, and these are summarised in Table 4.3. I also present explanations in cases where scholars gave them.

Again, participants are identified by number and country of work only. For example, CLT6 Australia, indicates the comment was made by Chinese Language Teacher 6, country of work Australia, and the abbreviation CLT16 China refers to Chinese Language Teacher 16, country of

Table 4.3 Selection of most and least important component of language comprehensive competitiveness from scholar interviews

Component of language comprehensive competitiveness	Times selected as most important	Times selected as least important
Policy competitiveness	0	0
Cultural competitiveness	0	1
Economic competitiveness	1	0
Population competitiveness	0	0
Script competitiveness	0	2
Scientific/technological competitiveness	0	0
Educational competitiveness	0	0
Geostrategic competitiveness	2	0

work China. Chinese scholars are identified by the abbreviation CS and a number, as in CS1.[6]

4.4   POLICY COMPETITIVENESS

Policy competitiveness received an average rating of 5.29 from Chinese language learners. Their comments indicate their awareness that Chinese is used in government bodies and international organisations, and the perception that Chinese would be useful for joining or interacting with them. Some typical comments are presented here:

> I want to work for DFAT [Department of Foreign Affairs and Trade], which requires a language, with Chinese being one of the main ones (CLL9 Australia).
> Many Asia-Pacific and East Asia regional institutions exist, with China becoming a central actor, the use of Chinese as a transactional language is important (CLL13 Australia).
> Chinese is one of the official languages of the United Nations, and has been identified as a good language to know when applying for Australian government jobs in defence and foreign affairs—since these are the types of careers I hope to enter, I thought learning Chinese would be a great advantage (CLL18 Australia).
> My major is international relations and a lot of institutions and organisations in my field require Chinese (CLL28 China).

Only one Chinese language teacher (CLT26 China) selected policy competitiveness as the most important component of language compre-hensive competitiveness for learners' decision to learn Chinese. CLT26 China explained that this was because the most conscientious students they had taught were those who were required by their governments to learn Chinese. This same participant also said that economic competi-tiveness and educational competitiveness were the second and third most important components, respectively.

Policy competitiveness was mentioned as an additional reason for learning Chinese (along with cultural and economic competitiveness) by one other CLT participant who selected geostrategic competitiveness as the most important (CLT16 China). None of the Chinese scholars iden-tified this component of language comprehensive competitiveness as the most important or least important.

Given its average rating from CLLs and limited backing from CLTs and CSs, policy competitiveness offers medium support for the macroacquisition of Chinese from the subjective perspective.

4.5 Cultural Competitiveness

Results for cultural competitiveness are interesting. This component received an average rating of 6.44, suggesting that culture is a reasonably important factor in learners' decision to acquire Chinese. There were indeed comments to this effect, such as CLL72 Australia who was "fascinated by Chinese culture and tradition". CLL65 Australia likewise said, "Chinese culture is very beautiful [and] full of tradition".

However, most comments indicate that while learners appreciate Chinese culture, it was not as important to them as other components. The following are indicative of learners' views:

I do love Chinese culture, but job prospects were the main reason for learning Chinese (CLL9 Australia).
Not a motivating factor for me personally, although I do respect this [Chinese culture] greatly (CLL10 Australia).
I enjoy Chinese culture, but I wouldn't say it is my primary reason [for learning Chinese] (CLL19 Australia).

Two CLT participants said cultural competitiveness was the most important component of language comprehensive competitiveness. It is interesting to note, however, that both also mentioned additional components, namely economic and geostrategic competitiveness. CLT10 Australia explained why they chose cultural competitiveness as well as economic competitiveness:

The students that I am teaching are really interested in knowing, understanding and appreciating Chinese traditional and contemporary culture, and learning Chinese language definitely helps them with not only comprehending Chinese philosophy but also expanding their thinking and wisdom; in addition, lots of my current students said that they would like to work and live in China when they finish [their] study, and some of my previous students are studying and working in China now.

CLT14 Australia distinguished between the different groups of learners they had taught, explaining that "mature [age] distance students" mostly learn Chinese because of interest in Chinese culture, China's importance in the world and China's economy. Recent high school graduates by contrast were "less aware of China's cultural tradition" and instead saw "Chinese proficiency as a helpful asset in a future career".

One also mentioned cultural competitiveness as the least important component after script competitiveness (CLT17 China). This participant explained that learners from different countries placed different emphasis on culture as a reason for learning Chinese:

> Of course, students from different countries have different thoughts. The geopolitical relations between China and the countries around it are quite complex; students' interests in learning Chinese are often motivated by practical benefits. But for the US and European countries, I've met many students who are purely interested in the Chinese language but have little concern about what practical benefits Chinese can bring them.

In a somewhat similar comment, CS3 said culture was the least important component of language comprehensive competitiveness:

> A small number of scholars are of course interested in culture, but they are the elite. People like Sinologists who specialise in China may learn Chinese for culture. Culture appeals to the elite, but you need economic power to appeal to the general public. Kungfu and food appeal to people a bit but not enough to learn Chinese – maybe they only pick up a few sentences or words.

Like policy competitiveness, cultural competitiveness offers medium support for macroacquisition.

4.6   ECONOMIC COMPETITIVENESS

Economic competitiveness received one of the highest average ratings of any component of language comprehensive competitiveness, with 7.21. Learners' comments show they see acquiring Chinese as a way to benefit from China's economy:

> I think China's economic influence is only starting to be the world player that it will be for a long time. So, for me to learn about China and the language used I envisage to be a wise decision down the track (CLL10 Australia).

Very important in the sense that clients may be Chinese and may not speak English, so I need to be able to communicate with them (CLL22 Australia).
China is very economically significant for Australia and learning the language is a way to capitalise on this (CLL24 Australia).
The economic power of China has the chance to beat the economic power of America (CLL47 China).
China's business is booming and growing faster than ever (CLL64 Australia).

The importance of economic competitiveness was also evident in the email interview responses from learners. In this example, CLL7 Australia discusses the employment opportunities created by China's economic growth in response to the question *Do you think the ability to speak Chinese will become more important in the future? Why/why not?*:

Yes, I do because China's economy has been developing rapidly over the past couple decades and I think it will grow even more. This will put Chinese to a good use because there will be more demand for people who can speak Chinese. Be it a translator or interpreter, or many other kinds of jobs.

CLL8 Australia also highlighted China's economic influence and linked this to other areas in which China has an impact on the world:

The ability to speak Chinese will become more important in the future. Economic interactions and inter-dependency between not only China and Australia but also Australia's allies will require more English speakers to be able to communicate in Chinese. Considering factors such as China's size both economically and demographically, globalisation, student exchange, engineering and technological advances and Asia-Pacific security, the ability to speak Chinese will become more important in the future.

CLL17 Australia gave another similar response:

With China's increased economic expansion globally, Chinese language ability will definitely be an advantage in terms of trade and employment.

CLL11 Australia was very clear about the primary importance of Chinese in the economic domain in answer to the question, *Do you think it is important for foreigners (i.e. people from non-Chinese backgrounds) to be able to speak Chinese? Why/why not?:*

> Yes, if you are in business. No, otherwise. For business, obviously since China's economy is growing, more profit can be gained by interacting with Chinese businesses. As for other foreigners who aren't interested in business, Chinese won't be relevant if you're not interested in China.

A total of 18 CLT participants selected economic competitiveness as the most important component of language comprehensive competitiveness in their learners' decision to learn Chinese, far more than any other component. Two of these also mentioned geostrategic competitiveness (CLT5 Australia and CLT17 China). The following are indicative of the kinds of comments made by CLT participants:

> The students [are] eager to understand more about this rapidly developing economy so as to find job opportunities relating to China in the future (CLT6 Australia).
>   I reckon this is a 'cornerstone' reason. Each semester when I started the lectures for the non-background beginner class, I also have asked students this question, why do you study Chinese? My general impression is that they felt Chinese is becoming more and more important because China's growing economic power implies increasing opportunities for their future. Of course, some said they were obsessed with Chinese culture. But the spreading of Chinese culture still heavily relies on mainland China's economic power. Think about three decades ago, people might learn Chinese but more so traditional Chinese and Cantonese. At that moment, Taiwan and Hong Kong carried out the more influential role in promoting Chinese culture and language (CLT9 Australia).

One CS participant nominated economic competitiveness as the most important component of language comprehensive competitiveness. CS3 said:

> Economic and commercial development is the motivation for governments to do business with China and access China's market. For individuals, lots of jobs are associated with the economy, so Chinese gives a competitive edge in the employment market.

This reflects the views and opinions of CLLs and CLTs that knowing Chinese can give one better employment opportunities and monetary benefits. Economic competitiveness clearly provides strong support for the macroacquisition of Chinese.

4.7   POPULATION COMPETITIVENESS

Population competitiveness was also rated very highly by learners, with an average rating of 7.32. Learners' comments demonstrate that they see Chinese as a language that can connect them to a vast number of people in different parts of the world, and that the Chinese diaspora is an important aspect of this:

> My main reason for studying Chinese is the number of Chinese speakers (CLL1 Australia).
> The expanding Chinese population and Chinese speakers may connect more countries that do not speak the same language (CLL12 Australia).
> Chinese people represent a large, if not the largest, diaspora throughout the world. Chinese is therefore widely spoken throughout the world (CLL17 Australia).
> One of the main reasons I began learning Chinese is its huge geographic spread (from China to Hong Kong, Taiwan, Singapore and Southeast Asia to diaspora communities in Australia); it means knowing the language gives access to many countries, cultures and peoples (CLL18 Australia).

Responses to the email interview also show the importance of population competitiveness as a driver of the macroacquisition of Chinese. CLL4 Australia, for example, made two comments pertinent to this component of language comprehensive competitiveness. This participant's answer to the question, *Do you think the ability to speak Chinese will become more important in the future? Why/why not?*, was:

> I think the ability to speak Chinese will be more important in the future due to China's growing population and its growing relationship with Australia.

Similarly, their answer to the question, *Do you think it is important for foreigners (i.e. people from non-Chinese backgrounds) to be able to speak Chinese? Why/why not?*, also referenced China's population:

I've never really thought about that but I think it probably is important as due to China's population, being able to speak the language would be beneficial.

Other responses to the first of these email interview questions also discussed China's population:

I think the ability to speak any language is a door to parts of the world that are otherwise closed. The more people that speak that language, the bigger the opportunities you get from understanding it. More people speak Chinese than any other language so it makes sense to be able to communicate with more people where you can. I don't think the ability to speak Chinese will be "more" important in the future. In fact, I think it will be less important, because I think more people in China will learn English as China continues to develop. But I think it is important now and I think it is selfish to expect such a huge country and quantity of people to learn my language so they can communicate with me (CLL6 Australia).

Yes, I think it will. China's large population, combined with rapid economic growth, as well as the fact that there are large expat populations of Chinese throughout the world – all these things lead me to believe that Chinese is becoming one of the main global languages (CLL19 Australia).

Interestingly, none of the CLT or CS participants selected population competitiveness as the most important. This may be because they have encountered the argument that the number of speakers of a language does not in itself make it powerful and influential during their studies and/or research (see, for example, Crystal, 2003).

Due to its salience in the minds of learners, population competitiveness is another component of language comprehensive competitiveness which provides strong support for the macroacquisition of Chinese.

4.8   SCRIPT COMPETITIVENESS

Script competitiveness was rated at 5.08. While there were a small number of enthusiastic comments regarding the script, such as that from CLL12 Australia who said that "characters are interesting" and "could be useful for other Asian countries as well", CLL14 Australia who said "Chinese characters are fun to learn" and CLL75 Australia who said Chinese is a "very beautiful and meaningful language", the majority of comments expressed difficulty and/or frustration with characters. The following are indicative examples:

> I apparently find Chinese very hard to learn, especially the writing (CLL16 Australia).
> Very diverse; too complex; need time to understand (CLL34 China).
> Writing Chinese is difficult (CLL44 China).
> It's different from many languages (CLL54 China).

Learners also rated characters/writing as the most difficult aspect of learning Chinese (31 mentions), followed by tones (28 mentions), pronunciation (21 mentions), grammar (14 mentions) and other aspects of the language or its study (8 mentions).

No CLT participants selected script competitiveness as the most important component of language comprehensive competitiveness. In fact, 17 of them selected it as the least important. Their comments mirror those of learners in identifying the challenges posed by the character-based writing system:

> Most students consider Chinese written script to be the scariest thing in learning Chinese (CLT2 Australia).
> I think the written script is probably off-putting for many students rather than appealing and even if they think the script in interesting to learn to learn I don't think it would be seen as 'being able to be used for all purposes' (CLT4, Australia).
> This is always the one that stops students from taking Chinese courses (CLT7 Australia).
> The complexity of the script is seen as more of a problem than an advantage (CLT19 Australia).

Two of the three CS participants also selected script competitiveness as the least important component. CS1 said, "Chinese characters are difficult to learn", while CS2 explained that they knew people who could speak Chinese well but could not read or write. They highlighted this was the opposite of most foreign language learning situations where people can often read and write but have difficulty speaking.

Script competitiveness therefore offers only weak support for macroacquisition.

4.9   SCIENTIFIC/TECHNOLOGICAL COMPETITIVENESS

Scientific/technological competitiveness received the lowest average rating from CLLs with 4.95. Some learners were aware of China's advances in science and technology, such as CLL19 Australia who said, "China is increasingly moving from primary manufacturing industries to innovation, tertiary sector economic activity". CLL41 China said, "China has many sources and good technologies", while CLL47 China said, "the advance of China [increased] faster than another country". CLL74 Australia also commented that scientific/technological developments are "relevant to my degree" and "lead to pathways in China".

However, most learners did not see this component of language comprehensive competitiveness as important for their decision to acquire Chinese, as can be seen from these examples:

> I didn't think about this when I chose to study Chinese (CLL7 Australia).
> Not at all. Many developments seem to come from Korea (CLL46 China).
> Maybe in the art of copying things but not developing their own products (CLL66 Australia).
> Science and technology aren't really where my interests lie (CLL71 Australia).

None of the CLT or CS participants believed scientific/technological competitiveness was the most important component of language comprehensive competitiveness for learners' decision to learn Chinese. Four CLT participants said it was the least important component, and one of the CLT participants who nominated script competitiveness also mentioned scientific/technological competitiveness (CLT26 China). The following comments indicate views on this component:

> I have rarely heard the students I teach cite this as a motivation for learning Chinese (CLT14 Australia).
> China's scientific development maybe a reason [to learn Chinese], but at least for me personally, I haven't met any students who have come to China to study because of China's development in science and technology (CLT16 China).
> Very few students mention this [as a reason to learn Chinese] (CLT21 China).

The data together indicate scientific/technological competitiveness offers weak support for macroacquisition.

4.10   Educational Competitiveness

Educational competitiveness is another component of language comprehensive competitiveness which provides medium support for the macroacquisition of Chinese. It received an average rating of 5.25. There were some positive comments regarding education and/or research in China, such as this from CLL21 Australia:

> As an anthropology student, I would love to be able to study anthropology in a non-western institute to get a balanced view of cultural understandings. China has some prestigious anthropological departments for this.
> Another participant, CLL41 China, said:
> Chinese education is extremely good.

However, most comments suggest learners do not see China as a leading destination for education, nor do they see Chinese as a language through which education and knowledge can be pursued, as the examples below show:

> I live in Australia, so this seems irrelevant. I'm not planning on living in China any time soon (CLL11 Australia).
> Western countries are and for a long time will be the number one group in education. In any case, English will be used primarily (CLL25 China).
> Still much lower than in Western countries, the whole different education doesn't allow them to be creative and innovative (CLL26 China).
> I don't feel the current education system in China is very successful; too little room for creativity and independent thinking (CLL28 China).

None of the CLT or CS participants selected educational competitiveness as the most important component of language comprehensive competitiveness for learners' decision to learn Chinese. Seven CLT participants said it was the least important component, and their views are similar to those of learners:

> I would not reckon students had a very good knowledge of education and research in China before they chose the subject (CLT5 Australia).

So far, I have never heard from my students that they wanted to study in China because the quality of education and scholarly research in China are high, but they are happy to join some language and cultural courses in China (CLT10 Australia).

I don't think the quality of education and scholarly research in China have been considered very high (CLT15 Australia).

It is difficult to say whether China's education and research level is high or not. Maybe in some fields and in some universities, the level is higher than in some countries, but this is not the main reason [for people to learn Chinese]. Many foreign students come to China to study only to have economic relations with China (CLT22 China).

Educational competitiveness provides medium support for the macroacquisition of Chinese on the basis of the learner questionnaire and teacher and scholar interviews.

4.11   GEOSTRATEGIC COMPETITIVENESS

Geostrategic competitiveness received the highest average rating of 7.55. China's position in the world and its power and influence are important reasons for learning Chinese in participants' eyes, as shown by these comments:

China has always been important in world affairs (CLL8 Australia).

Through protests by my Chinese international friends at university against the Chinese government, I became aware of and very interested in the affairs of China. I am interested in the increasing role China is playing as both an economic superpower, and an influential cultural superpower within the world (CLL21 Australia).

The rising position of China in the world is undeniable at the present time. As a result, it becomes more important to learn Chinese as a means to get involved in China's world affairs (CLL23 Australia).

Learning Chinese is a pragmatic measure: the Chinese influence in the world is growing, so speaking Chinese is a good start to understand China (CLL34 China).

China was a world leader before the Western world and China is again now a world leader. Most importantly, China retained its culture (CLL70 Australia).

Again, learner responses to the email interviews showed the importance of geostrategic competitiveness. For example, CLL18 Australia responded to the question, *Do you think the ability to speak Chinese will become more important in the future? Why/why not?*, by saying:

> I think that the likely continued rise of China's economic and political stature will make the ability to speak at least some Chinese ever more important, not only for people directly involved with Chinese businesses or in diplomacy but just to understand more about the world's largest economy and a country of over a billion people. As China becomes more globalised and its cultural exports more prominent, having a basic understanding of Chinese may be necessary in many aspects of life.

CLL20 Australia was more cautious, but still expressed a similar view in response to this question:

> Yes, I think that speaking Chinese will become more important as China grows as a world power. However, I'm not convinced that this will happen very quickly - so this is not really a reason that influenced my decision to study Chinese.

In response to the question, *Do you think it is important for foreigners (i.e. people from non-Chinese backgrounds) to be able to speak Chinese? Why/why not?*, CLL8 Australia said:

> I also feel that there will inevitably be a shift in power to China and diplomacy will be much easier if foreigners can speak Chinese.

Nine CLT participants and two CS participants agreed that geostrategic competitiveness was the most important component of language comprehensive competitiveness. Some indicative comments include:

> More and more of our students have come to know China better than their parents as China is no longer a myth but a real global stage player in all aspects. Many young Australians today would not only like to tour the country but also like to study, work and live in the country (CLT11 Australia).
> This [China's importance in the world] is highlighted a lot in the Australian press and is an important influence in decision making (CLT19 Australia).

One scholar also identified geostrategic competitiveness as the most important component, with similar reasoning:

China is emerging as a world power, and people believe Chinese brings cutting edge advantages for a future career. People hear more about China and see more about China; this promotes this view (CS2).

Interestingly, CLT9 Australia said geostrategic competitiveness was the least important component of language comprehensive competitiveness because:

It is too vague to link this with our students' motivation in learning Chinese. Even [though] China is playing a more significant role in the international arena, for western students, they could supposedly use English to understand China and communicate with Chinese regarding international affairs. This reason does not warrant their incentive to learning such a hard East Asian language.

This view was clearly in the minority one however.

Geostrategic competitiveness most obviously provides strong support for the macroacquisition of Chinese.

4.12   Conclusion

In this chapter, I examined the macroacquisition of Chinese from the subjective perspective. This complements the previous chapter by showing the language beliefs/ideology surrounding this phenomenon. The results of the questionnaire and interviews suggest that geostrategic competitiveness, population competitiveness and economic competitiveness are the components of language comprehensive competitiveness which most strongly support macroacquisition, while cultural competitiveness, policy competitiveness and educational competitiveness offer somewhat less support. Script competitiveness offers only limited support and scientific/technological competitiveness the least support for macroacquisition.

Notes

1. The full questionnaire is presented in Appendix 1.
2. The email interview questions are presented in Appendix 2.
3. Full demographic details of each Chinese language learner participant are presented in Appendix 3.
4. The interview questions for teachers are presented in Appendix 4.

5. The interview questions for scholars are presented in Appendix 5.
6. I have not identified any participants in this study for several reasons. Firstly, my university's ethics committee approved my project on the condition that all participants remain anonymous, and participants agreed to be part of the project with the understanding that they would not be identified. In addition, some of the participants were in China. Identifying people who live, study or work in China potentially puts them at risk because of the nature of the country's political system.

References

Crystal, D. (2003). *English as a global language* (2nd ed.). Cambridge University Press.
Hornberger, N. H., & Hult, F. M. (2008). Ecological language education policy. In B. Spolsky & F. M. Hult (Eds.), *The handbook of educational linguistics* (pp. 280–296). Blackwell Publishing.

CHAPTER 5

A Language Comprehensive Competitiveness Profile of Chinese

Abstract This chapter combines the findings of Chapters 3 and 4 to produce a language comprehensive competitiveness profile of Chinese. It categorises the components of language comprehensive competitiveness into strengths, weaknesses and intermediates. Geostrategic competitiveness, population competitiveness and economic competitiveness are strengths in the language comprehensive competitiveness profile of Chinese, while script competitiveness and scientific/technological competitiveness are weaknesses. Policy competitiveness, cultural competitiveness and educational competitiveness are neither clear strengths nor outright weaknesses and are therefore intermediates in the language comprehensive competitiveness profile of Chinese.

Keywords Chinese · Language comprehensive competitiveness · Profile

5.1 INTRODUCTION

Language comprehensive competitiveness is the association of a language with forms of power and resources that are valuable and bring benefits to its speakers within a language ecology. In this chapter, I present a language comprehensive competitiveness profile of Chinese. A profile, according to the *Cambridge English Dictionary*, is "a short description

© The Author(s), under exclusive license to Springer Nature   93
Switzerland AG 2021
J. Gil, *The Rise of Chinese as a Global Language*,
https://doi.org/10.1007/978-3-030-76171-4_5

of someone's life, work, character, etc." (Cambridge University Press, 2021). Profiles have been used to outline the use, status and characteristics of a particular language and its speakers, such as those in the *Ethnologue* database (Eberhard et al., 2020), to document the language use of multilingual people (see, for example, Chaudhry et al., 2010) and to describe the language skills and needs of second/additional language learners (see, for example, Council of Europe Language Policy Unit, 2020). Applied to language comprehensive competitiveness, a profile is a description of the extent to which each component supports macroacquisition.

Based on the findings presented in Chapters 3 and 4—summarised in Table 5.1—this profile groups the components of language comprehensive competitiveness into strengths, weaknesses and intermediates. In the strengths group are those components of language comprehensive competitiveness which offer strong support for macroacquisition from both the objective and subjective perspectives. The weaknesses group is made up of those components of language comprehensive competitiveness which offer limited support for macroacquisition from both the objective and subjective perspectives, or those components which provide very limited support from either the objective or subjective perspective. The intermediates group comprises those components which are neither clear strengths nor outright weaknesses for the macroacquisition of Chinese. These components support macroacquisition somewhat ambiguously from the objective, subjective or both perspectives.

Table 5.1 Degree of support for macroacquisition of components of language comprehensive competitiveness from the objective and subjective perspectives

Strong	Medium	Weak
Objective		
Geostrategic competitiveness	Policy competitiveness	Script competitiveness
Economic competitiveness	Cultural competitiveness	
Population competitiveness	Educational competitiveness	
	Scientific/technological competitiveness	
Subjective		
Geostrategic competitiveness	Cultural competitiveness	Script competitiveness
Population competitiveness	Policy competitiveness	Scientific/technological competitiveness
Economic competitiveness	Educational competitiveness	

I classify geostrategic competitiveness, population competitiveness and economic competitiveness as strengths. Policy competitiveness, cultural competitiveness and educational competitiveness are the components I group as intermediates. Finally, I consider the remaining two components of language comprehensive competitiveness, script competitiveness and scientific/technological competitiveness, as weaknesses.

5.2   STRENGTHS IN THE LANGUAGE COMPREHENSIVE COMPETITIVENESS PROFILE OF CHINESE

There are three components of language comprehensive competitiveness which offer strong support for macroacquisition. These are geostrategic competitiveness, population competitiveness and economic competitiveness.

Geostrategic competitiveness, when viewed from the objective and subjective perspectives, provides strong support for macroacquisition. China's interests in and connections with the world are significant, and learners, teachers and scholars felt this was an important reason for learning Chinese. This component received the highest average rating on the learner questionnaire and many comments in email interviews indicated its importance as a reason for learning Chinese.

Population competitiveness also strongly supports the macroacquisition of Chinese from the objective and subjective perspectives. This is not surprising given the number of speakers of all varieties of Chinese and the number of learners of Mandarin. This was very important to learners (second-highest average rating on the questionnaire and several comments in the email interviews), although less so to teachers and scholars.

Economic competitiveness strongly supports the macroacquisition of Chinese from both the objective and subjective perspectives. This is evident from the secondary data on China's economic development, its average rating on the questionnaire (third highest), comments on email interviews and its nomination by teachers and scholars as the most important component.

5.3   WEAKNESSES IN THE LANGUAGE COMPREHENSIVE COMPETITIVENESS PROFILE OF CHINESE

There are two components in this group, script competitiveness and scientific/technological competitiveness.

Script competitiveness offers weak support for the macroacquisition of Chinese from both the objective and subjective perspectives. This is due to the issues related to the character-based script and its perceived difficulty in the minds of participants. Comments from learners, teachers and scholars for the most part indicate it is an obstacle for learning the language, although it did not receive the lowest average rating on the questionnaire.

From the objective perspective, the scientific/technological competitiveness of Chinese is increasing as China develops its capabilities in this area. However, responses to the questionnaire suggest it is not important for the macroacquisition of Chinese from the subjective perspective (eighth-highest average rating). Teachers and scholars were likewise sceptical of its influence on learners' decision to acquire Chinese.

5.4   INTERMEDIATES IN THE LANGUAGE COMPREHENSIVE COMPETITIVENESS PROFILE OF CHINESE

Cultural competitiveness, policy competitiveness and educational competitiveness offer medium support for the macroacquisition of Chinese.

Cultural competitiveness supports macroacquisition from the objective perspective. Chinese culture is well known around the world and certain aspects of it are very popular. Chinese also has a growing presence on the Internet and in other media. From the subjective perspective, however, it was not considered as important as geostrategic, population and economic competitiveness by learners (fourth highest average rating), or teachers and scholars. In fact, some comments from all these participants explicitly stated it lacked the importance of other components.

The secondary data on government policies towards Chinese and the use of Chinese in international organisations shows that it has a limited role outside of the areas where it is spoken natively. Policies supporting the use of Chinese were somewhat important to learners as shown by this component receiving the fifth-highest average rating on the learner questionnaire and learners' and teachers' comments about its connections to employment opportunities.

Table 5.2 Language comprehensive competitiveness profile of Chinese

Strengths	Weaknesses	Intermediates
Geostrategic competitiveness	Script competitiveness	Cultural competitiveness
Population competitiveness	Scientific/technological competitiveness	Policy competitiveness
Economic competitiveness		Educational competitiveness

From the objective perspective, educational competitiveness can be considered a growing strength of Chinese. However, this was not matched from the subjective perspective. Educational competitiveness received the sixth-highest average rating, and most of the comments from participants were dismissive of this component.

These three components therefore provide only medium support for the macroacquisition of Chinese.

This language comprehensive competitiveness profile of Chinese is summarised in Table 5.2.

5.5 Conclusion

The language comprehensive competitiveness profile of Chinese presented in this chapter shows at a glance the driving forces of the macroacquisition of the language. The most obvious strengths in this profile are geostrategic, population and economic competitiveness, with cultural, policy and educational competitiveness representing neither clear strengths nor outright weaknesses. Script and scientific/technological competitiveness are the most significant weaknesses in the language comprehensive competitiveness profile of Chinese.

This profile provides the basis for a discussion of the implications of the macroacquisition of Chinese for the future of English as a global language. Xu (2007) argues that Chinese would need to be appealing to learners across all the components of language comprehensive competitiveness in order for it to achieve global language status. In a similar vein, several other scholars have also argued that Chinese lacks some of the key requirements of a global language (see for example Bruthiaux, 2002; Lu, 2008). In particular, the written script has been a major issue in the debate about the possible future of Chinese. In the next chapter, I look at the role of the character-based script in detail to show it will not necessarily prevent Chinese becoming a global language.

Developments in policy, cultural, scientific/technological and educational competitiveness are likely to take considerable time and be dependent on the outcome of China's rise. In Chapter 7, I explore various scenarios for the future of Chinese and English as global languages in light of how China's rise may pan out.

REFERENCES

Bruthiaux, P. (2002). Predicting challenges to English as a global language in the 21st century. *Language Problems & Language Planning, 26*(2), 129–157.

Cambridge University Press. (2021). Profile. In *Cambridge English dictionary*. Cambridge University Press. Retrieved 19 February, 2021, from https://dictionary.cambridge.org/dictionary/english/profile?q=Profile

Chaudhry, S., Khan, M., & Mahay, A. (2010). A multilingual family's linguistic profile in Manchester: A domain analysis of English, Urdu and Punjabi. *Multilingual Manchester Report 2010*. Retrieved 19 February, 2021, from http://mlm.humanities.manchester.ac.uk/wp-content/uploads/2015/12/Linguistic-profile-of-a-multilingual-family.pdf

Council of Europe Language Policy Unit. (2020). *Linguistic profiles and profiling*. Retrieved 17 February, 2021, from https://www.coe.int/en/web/lang-migrants/profile-language-/-profiling

Eberhard, D. M., Simons, G. F., & Fennig, C. D. (Eds.). (2020). *Ethnologue: Languages of the World* (23rd ed.). Retrieved 19 February, 2021, from http://www.ethnologue.com

Lu, D. (2008). Pre-imperial Chinese: Its hurdles towards becoming a world language. *Journal of Asian Pacific Communication, 18*(2), 268–279.

Xu, J. (2007). 语言规划与语言教育 *Language planning and language education*. Xuelin Press.

CHAPTER 6

The Role of the Character-Based Writing System in the Future Global Dynamics of Chinese

Abstract This chapter takes issue with the common argument that Chinese cannot replace English as a global language because of its character-based written script. It shows that this argument is based on flawed assumptions about proficiency, lack of recognition of the use of technology in the learning and use of characters, unawareness of the historical precedent for the adoption of characters outside of China and excessive focus on linguistic properties. Should conditions prove right, a character-based writing system will not prevent Chinese from becoming a global language.

Keywords Characters · Chinese · Future of Chinese as a global language · Future of English as a global language · Global language · Written script

6.1 INTRODUCTION

Ascertaining the role of the character-based writing system is a key aspect of understanding the future global dynamics of Chinese. The prevailing view among scholars and commentators is that such a writing system will prevent Chinese from becoming a global language because it is difficult and time-consuming to learn. There are undoubtedly challenges involved in learning and using characters, and these have been well-documented (see, for example, Moser, 1991). But is a character-based writing system really inimical to global language status?

In this chapter, I present four counter-arguments to the prevailing view. Firstly, I argue this view is based on the flawed assumption that all learners of Chinese must learn to read and write, and must do so to a native-like level. This does not reflect the global use of English, as not everyone can read and write, and certainly not to a native-like level. People learn as much English as is required for their purposes, and the same would apply if Chinese was to become a global language. Next, I argue this view ignores the use of devices like computers and mobile phones which convert Pinyin Romanisation into characters, meaning learners need only learn Pinyin and character recognition, thus saving considerable time and effort. Thirdly, I show there is a historical precedent for the adoption of characters outside of China in the form of the long-standing use of written Chinese for scholarly and official purposes in Korea, Japan and Vietnam. This occurred due to China's status as the most powerful country in the region, if not the world, and demonstrates people will learn and use characters if there is sufficient reason to do so. Finally, I argue this view focuses excessively on linguistic properties. The inconsistencies and irregularities of English's writing system show linguistic properties do not determine whether a language becomes global. I conclude that a character-based writing system will not, in and of itself, prevent Chinese attaining global language status.

6.2   WHY CHARACTERS ARE STILL USED

For over a century now, there have been tensions in China between viewing characters as a problem and viewing them as an essential aspect of Chinese culture that cannot be done away with, and these have played out against the backdrop of important political and social events. In pre-modern China, characters, and writing in general, were very highly regarded. As Gottlieb and Chen (2001) explain, "script was taken to be sacrosanct by the general public, to the extent that many people would not dare to step on a piece of paper with characters written on it" (p. 6). For scholars and officials, who gained their positions through mastery of the written language and classic philosophical and literary works, the character-based writing system was seen as superior to all others. They certainly knew about, and some even studied, the phonetic scripts used to write Uyghur, Tibetan, Mongolian and Sanskrit, but believed people who used such scripts lacked the sophistication of the Chinese (DeFrancis, 1950).

A drastic reconsideration of the writing system and its role in society was sparked by China's clashes with Western countries, beginning with the Opium War of 1839–1842. For most of the time since the script was invented, Chinese was written in a traditional literary style of language called 文言 *wényán* (literally meaning "text-based speech").[1] It was used for writing about subjects such as history and philosophy, as well as technical writing and most literature, and was also the language of administration. *Wényán* was very different from the spoken language, due to its economy of expression, lack of punctuation and heavy use of literary allusions, and required many years of dedicated study to learn. As most Chinese people lacked the time and resources to do so, the vast majority of the population were unable to read or write, and could only speak their native dialects (Norman, 1988; Taylor & Taylor, 2014). Reform of the writing system, together with the development of a national standard spoken language, was seen as essential to modernise and develop the country. Scholars and officials such as Huang Zunxian and Qiu Tingliang called for *wényán* to be replaced by 白话 *báihuà* (literally meaning "plain speech"), a vernacular literary language used since the Tang and Song dynasties for popular novels such as *Journey to the West* and *Dream of the Red Chamber*, and lexico-grammatically much closer to the everyday spoken language. This suggestion was applied during the Qing dynasty's Reform Movement of 1898, and resulted in the use of *báihuà* for a considerable number of newspapers, magazines and textbooks, although some strong opposition remained among sections of the intelligentsia and the literati (Chen, 1999).

Efforts to reform the writing system were given extra impetus during the Republican era, when prominent writers and intellectuals such as Hu Shi and Chen Duxiu argued the case for *báihuà*. Some advocates of writing reform went even further, arguing that characters should be replaced with a phonetic script. For those like Qian Xuantong and Fu Sinian, switching to *báihuà* was not enough to make the written language easily accessible and enable widespread literacy and education (Chen, 1999; Moser, 2016). However, as DeFrancis (1950) points out, such views were in the minority, and the bulk of opinion at the time favoured maintaining characters. The *báihuà* movement was very successful; by 1920, the Ministry of Education had prescribed that all textbooks must be written in *báihuà* and *báihuà* must be taught in the first two years of primary school. *Wényán* was still used to some extent in government documents, business correspondence and some journalism into the 1940s, but *báihuà* had essentially taken over as the vehicle of written Chinese (Chen, 1999; Norman, 1988).

Attempts to adopt a phonetic script instead of characters, on the other hand, achieved only limited success. A number of phonetic scripts had in fact been developed by Western missionaries from the sixteenth century onwards and by Chinese from the late nineteenth century. Some of these enjoyed brief periods of popularity in certain areas of the country and even some official support, most notably 官话字母 (*guānhuà zìmǔ*, Mandarin Phonetic Alphabet), invented by Wang Zhao in 1900 and later revised by Lao Naixuan to cover Wu, Cantonese and Min in addition to Mandarin. Over 60,000 books were published in the Mandarin Phonetic Alphabet on topics ranging from history to zoology, and dozens of schools were established to teach it, usually by wealthy Chinese women who wanted to encourage literacy among women and girls, or provincial officials who saw literacy as necessary for increasing the efficiency and effectiveness of their armies and workforces. However, attempts by its creators to have it endorsed by the national government became mired in bureaucracy, and were unsuccessful (Chen, 1999; DeFrancis, 1950).

In 1913, the Conference on the Unification of Pronunciation gave serious consideration to the development of a phonetic script, and produced the 注音字母 *zhùyīn zìmǔ*, or Phonetic Alphabet, consisting of 39 symbols based on Chinese characters. It was promulgated by the Ministry of Education in 1918 along with a statement that it was to be used to facilitate the learning of characters, rather than to replace them (Chen, 2001). According to Chen (1999), it proved useful in demonstrating and promoting the pronunciation of the national standard language in the ensuing years up until the 1949 revolution. It remains in use in Taiwan today under the name 注音符號 *zhùyīn fúhào* (Moser, 2016).

There was also interest in simplifying characters. Scholars submitted a list of more than 2000 simplified characters based mainly on shorthand versions to the Ministry of Education for its consideration, and in August 1935 the Ministry issued a reduced list of 324 simplified frequently used characters for use in schools and publications. This was withdrawn just six months later due to intense opposition from some government figures, chief among them the Minister of Personnel Supervision, Dai Jitao. Dai argued that simplification would result in the loss of China's cultural heritage and separate people from the knowledge and traditions contained in material written in the past (Zhao & Baldauf, 2011, 2012).

The Chinese Communist Party (CCP) was interested in script reform even before it came to power, and decided on a policy of using an alphabetic script instead of characters. According to proponents of script reform in the CCP, "Chinese characters were a product of the old feudal society, and had become a tool with which the ruling class oppressed the labouring masses", and were considered "an insurmountable impediment to higher literacy, and so unsuitable for a modern society" (Chen, 1999, p. 186). The CCP had some success with this during its Yan'an period, when it adopted a system called *Latinxua Sin Wenz*, or Latinised New Writing, invented by Chinese immigrants to the Soviet Union in cooperation with Soviet linguists. Its proponents believed each dialect should have its own alphabetic script, and no fewer than 13 versions of Latinised New Writing were developed to cover the major dialects (Chen, 1999). Some 300 publications and a pocket dictionary were produced, and it was taught to children (Moser, 2016).

Reforming the writing system was considered so important that the Chinese Script Reform Association was established on the same day as the People's Republic of China (PRC), on 1 October 1949. Between 1950 and 1958, more than 1700 scripts were proposed. However, the CCP changed its policy and instead decided to simplify characters rather than replace them, and develop a phonetic script as an aid for learning characters only. The likely reasons for this were opposition from intellectuals and the literati, more pressing concerns facing the CCP at the time, and Stalin's suggestion to Mao Zedong during his visit to the Soviet Union that China should not use the Roman alphabet but a uniquely Chinese script (DeFrancis, 2006; Rohsenow, 2004).

In 1956 the State Council issued the Scheme of Simplified Chinese Characters, containing simplified versions of 515 characters and 54 radicals. The General List of Simplified Characters appeared in 1964, containing 2236 characters consisting of all of those in the 1956 scheme and characters which contained its simplified radicals. Simplification was conducted mainly on the principles of adopting shorthand versions of characters already in use among the public, reviving older versions of characters with less complex forms than their modern versions, removing certain parts of characters altogether, replacing parts of characters with simpler parts with the same pronunciation, and where possible, using a single character for a number of words with the same pronunciation (Chen, 1999; Ramsey, 1987). The main effect of the simplification process was to reduce the number of strokes in characters. According to Zhao and Baldauf (2011), the number of strokes in the simplified characters was reduced from 16 to 10.3 on average.

Further simplification was attempted in 1977. Work on the Second Simplification Scheme commenced during the chaotic years of the Cultural Revolution (1966–1976), and as such was heavily influenced by the radical politics of the time rather than sound linguistic and technical principles. It consisted of around 100 shorthand versions of characters, 853 simplified characters, 61 simplified radicals and 263 characters which were to be replaced by homophones. A trial implementation of 248 of these characters in the media was greeted with resistance and criticism from the public and linguists alike, and was soon abandoned. It was officially repealed at the National Conference on Language and Script Work in 1986. The General List of Simplified Characters was reissued in the same year with only minor changes, and some characters were returned to their original form (Rohsenow, 2004; Zhao & Baldauf, 2011).[2]

Traditional characters made something of a comeback in the 1980s, spurred by the renewed interest in traditional customs and cultural practices which had been repressed and criticised during the Cultural Revolution, made possible by the easing of political constraints and the opening of society. Traditional characters appeared on shops signs, name cards and reprints of books and other materials written before simplification. Some of the proposed simplified characters from the 1977 list were also taken up by some members of the public (Kane, 2006). Most significantly, a group of prominent and politically connected individuals, led by Yuan Xiaoyuan, a returned overseas Chinese woman, went as far as to argue traditional characters should be reintroduced. Zhao (2005) calls this group the Chinese Character Culture Faction (CCCF) because they believed the traditional characters best represented Chinese culture, possessed aesthetic beauty, encoded and transmitted information better than other scripts and bestowed cognitive advantages. They established an academic journal, *Chinese Character Culture*, and a research institute, the International Chinese Character Research Association, to pursue their agenda (Guo, 2004). At roughly the same time, developments in technology raised new issues regarding how characters could be digitised to enable Chinese to be used in computing systems and later cyberspace (Zhao, 2010).

There appears to have been some sympathy towards the CCCF position in the government as its emphasis on the uniqueness and superiority of characters was in line with the government's patriotic education campaign to encourage loyalty to China and minimise Western cultural and ideological influence among the population following the large-scale student protests of the 1980s (Guo, 2004; Zhao, 2005). Some high ranking government and Party figures attended events held by the International Chinese Character Research Association, and traditional character versions of important official publications such as *People's Daily* and *Outlook* were launched in the mid-1980s, targeted primarily at overseas Chinese populations (Guo, 2004).

However, the main thrust of the government's response from this time has been to focus on maintaining the use of officially sanctioned simplified characters and digitising characters. For example, the Language Law of 2001 emphasised the use of standardised characters over unofficial or informal versions, and permitted the use of traditional characters only for historical relics and sites, artistic works, handwritten characters on inscriptions and signs, variant characters in personal names and when required for teaching, research and publications (Rohsenow, 2004). Later, in 2009, the List of Standard Common Characters was released with the main aim of setting characters for personal names, place names and scientific and technical terms, particularly for use in computer input systems (Premaratne, 2012; Zhao & Baldauf, 2012).

As characters were being simplified, a Romanisation system for writing Chinese phonetically, 汉语拼音 *hànyǔ pīnyīn*, literally meaning "Chinese spelled sounds", was also developed. Commonly referred to simply as Pinyin, this system consists of symbols from the Roman alphabet and is based on the Beijing dialect of Mandarin. Its intended purpose is to facilitate learning of characters for all Chinese speakers and the learning of the pronunciation of Modern Standard Chinese for speakers of non-Mandarin dialects. It has been used in the PRC since 1958, and is also the main Romanisation scheme used internationally, having been accepted by the International Standardisation Organisation (ISO) as the means for transcribing Chinese in 1982 (Chen, 1999; Ramsey, 1987; Rohsenow, 2004). The National Conference on Language and Script Work of 1986 declared that there would be no further moves towards phonetisation of the writing system, confining Pinyin to these auxiliary roles (Zhao & Baldauf, 2011).

A widely held perception throughout all the eras discussed here that has worked against the replacement of characters is that a phonetic writing system is not suitable for Chinese because of its large number of homophonous morphemes and words. Kirkpatrick (2010) gives the example of *jī*, which can have thirty-five different meanings. In speaking these are not problematic because the context makes clear what is being talked about, but in writing, where such contextual clues are reduced or missing completely, homophones can only be distinguished by using different characters.

In addition, the same written script is used all over China, so regardless of which dialect one speaks, the written script can generally be understood.[3] As discussed above, adopting a phonetic script implies different scripts for each dialect. The fact that characters are not truly phonetic also means people can read very old texts such as Tang dynasty poetry and the works of Confucius, at least to some extent. This cannot be done with a language with a phonetic script because the sounds of the language, and therefore their representation in writing, would have changed considerably since the time the text was written. Characters have therefore provided Chinese people with a sense of unity and the nation with a sense of continuity with its past (Chen, 2007; Taylor & Taylor, 2014). The issue of unity has arguably become more important and sensitive in the current political environment under President Xi Jinping.

There have been no further serious attempts to replace characters with a phonetic script, making it very likely characters will continue to be used for the foreseeable future at least.

6.3   WHY CHARACTERS WILL NOT PREVENT CHINESE BECOMING A GLOBAL LANGUAGE

In the twenty-first century, the debate about characters has taken on a new dimension, focused on the future global status of Chinese. A review of academic and media sources shows the dominant view is that a character-based writing system will prevent Chinese from becoming a global language. To determine whether this is a sound argument, it is necessary to explore and analyse the language beliefs/ideologies which inform it, as well as draw implications from the current language practices associated with English as a global language for those likely to accompany Chinese should it become a global language.

6.3.1 Flawed Assumptions

The linguist John McWhorter (2015) says that "truly mastering the writing system virtually requires having been born to it". Similar views are expressed in the media, such as an article on the Voice of America (VOA) Learning English website which says Chinese has "a tone and writing system that is more difficult for adult learners to master" than other languages (Brock, 2014). Such statements assume everyone must learn to read and write, and must do so to a native-like level. However, this does not reflect the current situation and use of English. Not everyone can read and write, and certainly not to a native-like level.

While there are no definitive figures for levels of English language proficiency around the world, the Education First English Proficiency Index (EF EPI) does give a broad brush indication and is based on actual test results rather than estimates or impressions of proficiency, as is often the case. It is also regularly referenced by researchers working in the field of English language education. The 2020 EF EPI ranks 100 countries/regions from very high to very low levels of proficiency in English based on the EF Standard English Test results of more than 2.2 million participants. The EF Standard English Test is conducted online and covers reading and listening skills. While rankings are not broken into individual skills, the results as displayed in Table 6.1 show a cline of proficiency, with 12 countries in the very high group, 17 in the high group, 18 in the moderate group, 29 in the low group and 24 in the very low group, as defined by the Common European Framework of Reference (CEFR) levels (Education First, 2020).

Clearly, there are more countries/regions in the very low and low groups than the high and very high groups. Furthermore, as Mufwene (2013) points out, the use of English tends to be confined to certain domains and areas outside of Inner Circle countries. Its use is most obvious in tourism and international trade, and tends to be concentrated in urban areas. Beyond this, its use is limited. In Expanding Circle countries high levels of proficiency are needed only by those engaged in activities such as international business or travel. For the vast majority of the population, English is encountered and used only in school, and may well be "lost as quickly as that of various other subjects learned in school, which lack practical applications to the [students'] lives" (Mufwene, 2013, p. 49). Even in Outer Circle countries where English has intranational uses, it is confined mainly to white-collar professions, while the rest of

Table 6.1   Levels of English language proficiency worldwide

Proficiency band	Number of countries/regions	Example countries/regions	Example tasks/abilities at proficiency band
Very high	12	Netherlands Singapore Sweden	Use nuanced & appropriate language Read advanced texts Negotiate a contract
High	17	Kenya Philippines Switzerland	Make a work presentation Understand TV programmes Read newspapers
Moderate	18	China Italy Russia	Participate in meetings about one's area of expertise Understand lyrics of songs Write professional emails on familiar topics
Low	29	Japan Peru Indonesia	Find one's way around an English speaking country Participate in small talk Understand simple emails
Very low	24	Afghanistan Cambodia Angola	Introduce oneself by name, age & country of origin Understand basic signs Give basic directions

Source Compiled from data in Education First (2020)

the population function in the languages of the country in question (Mufwene, 2013). Fishman (2000) makes a similar point by reminding us that social class, age, gender and profession influence opportunities to acquire English and levels of attainment.

Yet English serves as a global language despite the fact not everyone possesses native or native-like proficiency. The reasons for varying degrees of proficiency are complex as hinted at above, but one important contributing factor is that people learn only as much English as is required for their purposes. As Edwards (2012) says, "except among those for whom repertoire expansion is a goal in and of itself, language competence typically extends only as far as current requirements dictate" (p. 28). The same would apply to Chinese as a global language.

To offer an example of such language practices, I observed a stallholder in Adelaide's Central Market call out to Chinese shoppers, "买菜,买菜" (*mǎi cài, mǎi cài*), which means "Buy vegetables, buy vegetables". It is unlikely the stallholder knows how to read or write the characters but there is no need to: he only needs enough Chinese to attract the attention (and money) of Chinese shoppers. Such language practices are similar to stallholders in markets in China who call out "Hello, look, look" to foreign tourists.

Even where reading and writing are necessary, not all learners will need to reach the same level of proficiency. A large Chinese dictionary would have 50,000 or more characters, but nowhere near that amount is required for what a learner (or a native speaker for that matter) might reasonably be expected to do. Table 6.2 shows the number of characters required for various purposes, ranging from limited literacy to scholarly, high-level literacy.

The amount of characters required will again depend on what a learner needs to do with the language. It should not be assumed that "mastery", with its implied native speaker level, is an appropriate goal or model for all learners. This notion has in fact been heavily critiqued and criticised in English language teaching and learning for more than two decades (see, for example, Canagarajah, 1999; Cook, 1999; Phillipson, 1992), so it is strange that it should be applied to discussions of Chinese as a potential global language.

Table 6.2 Characters required for various types of literacy

Purpose	Number of characters required
Scholarly, high level literacy	6000
Functional literacy	3500
Limited literacy	2000

Source Compiled from data in Taylor and Taylor (2014)

6.3.2   Technology and the Learning and Use of Characters

The difficulty of and time required to learn characters are often put forward as reasons why Chinese will not become a global language. A typical statement is expressed by Lu (2008) who says, "the complexity and difficulty of the writing system handicap its spread" (p. 268). He goes on to say "if the writing system of Chinese remains hard to learn for foreign learners, it will be hopeless for Chinese to become a world language" (p. 273). Ulrich Ammon says that although Chinese will increase in importance among the world's languages in the future, it is "difficult to read and write" (quoted in Noack, 2015). Martinez (2015) similarly argues that difficultly and time commitment will count against Chinese when he says, "the language is just too hard for outsiders to attain fluency in it[,] at least for outsiders who can't devote themselves full-time to memorizing thousands of characters over a number of years". MacKenzie (2018) echoes this sentiment when he says most people whose L1 is not related to Chinese "will find learning Mandarin an overly daunting prospect" because "learning to read Chinese involves learning several thousand characters" (p. 98) and substantial time to learn them.

The scope and scale of the task of learning characters should not of course be underestimated, as discussed in Chapter 3. However, technology has had a considerable impact on writing practices, and can make learning and using characters considerably easier and quicker for those learners who do need to do so. Computers, mobile phones and other electronic devices have software that converts Pinyin into characters. When Pinyin is typed, a character generation box will appear on the device with all the characters whose pronunciation matches the Pinyin, arranged in order of frequency of occurrence. The required character can then be selected. Entering two or more syllables at once usually expedites the process as it is clear what characters are needed from among the options available (Taylor & Taylor, 2014). For example, if one wants to write 你好, the Chinese word for "hello", which in Pinyin is rendered nǐ hǎo, one simply types the letters "ni" and the software will display all the characters which are pronounced "ni". One then selects the correct character. The process is repeated for "hao". Typing "nihao" as a single unit will bring up both characters together. This is arguably the dominant way of writing for Chinese speakers today.[4] In the context of debates about the possibility of Chinese becoming a global language, this means people need only learn Pinyin and character recognition, rather than character writing. This obviously saves much time and effort.

These same technologies make accessing learning materials easy and immediate. A YouTube search I conducted in December 2020 for "how to write Chinese characters" returned dozens of videos while a Google search returned 132,000,000 results. Mobile apps are another such source. The Chinese Characters First Steps app, developed by Open University, allows learners to look up the meaning, pronunciation and typical uses of characters in an online dictionary; use Pinyin to select and recognise characters; and test their knowledge of characters (Kan et al., 2018). All of these provide a richer and more varied environment for learning and using characters than what was available to learners prior to the development of such technologies.

There is already research on how technology can facilitate the learning and use of characters (see, for example, Kan et al., 2018; Levy & Steel, 2015; Shei & Hsieh, 2012), and this will likely grow as Chinese is added to the school and university curriculum around the world. This will in turn lead to improvements in teaching practice. Although the Chinese script may still take more time to learn than a phonetic one, sound teaching methods and quality teaching materials implemented by well-trained teachers can make this process far more efficient and effective.

6.3.3   A (Partial) Historical Precedent

Bruthiaux (2002) argues writing systems are one key factor in determining whether another language could replace English as a global language and sees this as particularly detrimental to the prospects for Chinese. He says the "continued reliance on a primarily logographic script is likely to limit the chances of Chinese as currently written acceding to a global role even in the likely event of a massive expansion of China's geopolitical clout in the coming decades" (p. 140). Robert Lane Greene, *The Economist*'s language correspondent, makes a similar argument: "As long as China keeps the character-based system—which will probably be a long time, thanks to cultural attachment and practical concerns alike— Chinese is very unlikely to become a true world language, an auxiliary language like English, the language a Brazilian chemist will publish papers in, hoping that they will be read in Finland and Canada" (Lane Greene, 2012). And Pullum (2016), in a piece titled "The awful Chinese writing system", poses the question "is the Chinese writing system a sufficient reason on its own to guarantee that Mandarin will not become a global language like English?", and answers in the affirmative. Dorren (2018), meanwhile, acknowledges Chinese will become more important in the future due to China's rise, but rules out the possibility that it will become a global language because it "is just too damn difficult" because of its "inefficient script" (p. 335). MacKenzie (2018) is equally direct in seeing the difficulty of learning the script as a significant obstacle, arguing it "would seem to count against Mandarin becoming a *written* global lingua franca [emphasis original]" (p. 98).[5]

Chinese has in fact been adopted by people outside of China before as a result of China's standing in the world. Scholars, officials and Buddhist monks in Korea, Japan and Vietnam used Chinese characters as their written lingua franca from roughly the third century to the second half of the twentieth century, as documented by Denecke (2014), Kornicki (2018) and Snow (2010). Its use and status were akin to Latin in medieval Europe, and as such these countries constituted what Denecke (2014) calls the "Sinographic Sphere" (p. 209). Chinese was used for reading and writing texts in the domains of administration, religion and high-brow literature (Denecke, 2014). Most interesting in light of claims that Chinese is unsuited to a global role is the phenomenon of 笔谈 *bǐtán*, "brush talk". Brush talk involved East Asian diplomats conducting face-to-face communication with their Chinese counterparts by writing characters down on paper. A shared spoken language was unnecessary because of the logographic nature of the Chinese script (Denecke, 2014). Clements (2019) shows brush talk was also practised during diplomatic interactions between Choson Korea and Tokugawa Japan from the seventeenth to nineteenth century.

Chinese was not used because of the merits of characters as a writing system, but because China was admired as the most advanced and civilised country, and these people desired to emulate China. This admiration of Chinese culture and civilisation was sufficient to prompt the learning and use of characters *despite* the difficulties involved. Of course, this is a somewhat limited precedent as the use of Chinese at this time was clearly not on the same scale as present-day English. Those who did use Chinese also employed various techniques to make the use of characters easier, such as notating texts with diacritic marks which indicated grammatical aspects of the native language and following the sentence structure of their native language when writing texts in characters (Denecke, 2014; Snow, 2010).

Nevertheless, it does demonstrate people will invest time and effort to learn and use characters if there is sufficient motivation to do so. China's economic and political importance could well provide such impetus today, a point I will return to later.

For now, it should also be noted that these past language practices have left a powerful legacy. With the exception of Vietnam which has used a Romanised writing system called *Quoc Ngu* since 1945 (Lo Bianco, 2001), these countries still use Chinese characters to some extent. Japanese uses Chinese characters (called *kanji* in Japanese) for the majority of its nouns as well as verb, adjective and adverb stems, and *hiragana* (a syllabary) for its affixes. Another syllabary, *katakana*, is used for foreign loan words and names. Both are based on the shapes of Chinese characters (Gottlieb, 2001). Some 2136 characters are taught in schools and approximately 3000 are used in newspapers, magazines and books (Gottlieb, 2012).

In the case of Korean, just over half of its vocabulary is originally from Chinese, and these words are partly written with Chinese characters (called *hanja* in Korean) in newspapers and journals in South Korea. Secondary school students are also expected to learn 1800 characters. In North Korea, the use of characters has been eliminated in everyday usage, but 3000 characters are still taught across secondary school, technical school and university to maintain comprehensibility of the script in case of reunification (King, 2007; Song, 2001). Learners who are literate in these languages will have the advantage of being familiar with many Chinese characters already.[6]

6.3.4   Focus on Linguistic Properties

A common thread running throughout all of the statements presented here is that they focus on the linguistic properties of Chinese. This idea is captured in Kirkpatrick's (2010) statement that "The major – perhaps the only – disadvantage that Chinese has is a linguistic one, namely the complexity of its script" (p. 15).[7] According to Araya (2012), "The writing system for Mandarin is arcane, and it consists of thousands of symbols rather than a simple alphabet", and this will greatly affect its chances of ever becoming a global language. Once again, there is a disconnect between these statements and what is known about how English became a global language. A basic tenet in this field of study is that the global status of a language is not determined on linguistic grounds, or

Table 6.3   Sound/spelling discrepancies in English

Discrepancy	Examples
A single sound can be represented by different letters	h*e*; bel*ie*ve; s*ee*; p*eo*ple; s*ei*ze; s*ea*; sill*y*; k*ey* where all words represent [i] with different letters
A single letter can represent different sounds	d*a*me [eɪ]; d*a*d [æ]; f*a*ther [a]; c*a*ll [ɔ]; vill*a*ge [ɪ]; m*a*ny [e]
A single sound can be represented by more than one letter	*sh*oot [ʃ]; *ch*aracter [tʃ]; *Th*omas [t]; *ph*ysics [f]; *dea*l [i]; c*oa*t [oʊ]
Some letters do not represent any sounds in a word	*wh*ole; resi*g*n; g*h*ost; lam*b*; i*s*land; *p*sychology
Some sounds do not have a specific letter to represent them	c*u*te; f*u*el; *u*se where 'u' is [ju]
A single letter can represent two sounds	bo*x*; sa*x*ophone where 'x' is [ks]

Source Compiled from data in Dobrovolsky (2011) and Fromkin et al. (2018)

what Crystal (2012) calls intrinsic linguistic factors. Claims that English become a global language because of its linguistic properties, such as its high number of loan words, minimal inflections or lack of grammatical gender, have been dismissed by scholars (see, for example, Crystal, 2003; Galloway & Rose, 2015).

It is also worth remembering that English has its own script problems due to considerable discrepancies between how English sounds and how it is spelled. One writer has described the English alphabet as having an "idiosyncratic and whimsical relation to pronunciation" (Dorren, 2018, p. 326). There are six such discrepancies, as shown in Table 6.3.

All of these make learning English as a second/additional language complicated. Yet, none of them stopped English becoming a global language for the simple reason that it is not the linguistic properties of a language that make it global, but the power and influence of the people who speak it and the countries in which it is spoken. Assuming China's power and influence continue to grow, it is reasonable to expect the use and status of Chinese will also expand, regardless of its linguistic features.

6.4   Conclusion

Much of the discussion about whether Chinese can become a global language while maintaining a character-based written script has shown flawed assumptions about proficiency, a lack of recognition of the use of technology in the learning and use of characters, unawareness of the historical precedent for the adoption of characters outside of China and excessive focus on linguistic properties. This is not to say that Chinese will become a global language any time soon; as I have argued elsewhere in this book, it is still a long way behind English. But, should conditions prove right, a character-based writing system will not prevent Chinese becoming a global language. This is the topic of the next chapter.

NOTES

1. I thank the anonymous reviewer of my article, "Will a character based writing system stop Chinese becoming a global language? A review and reconsideration of the debate", upon which this chapter is based, for suggesting "text-based speech" as an appropriate literal translation of *wényán*.

2. Whether simplification increased literacy remains open to debate. On the one hand, by the year 2010, over 95% of China's population aged 15 and over could read and write (World Bank, 2019), which represents a vast increase in literacy since the early twentieth century. However, Taiwan also has a very high literacy rate of 98.04% (Kuo, 2011), but did not undertake simplification.

3. Modern Written Chinese is based on the grammar and lexicon of Mandarin, and is therefore easier to understand for L1 speakers of Mandarin than for L1 speakers of other dialects (Chen, 1999). There are also some characters for words specific to Cantonese, and these are used for various purposes such as in newspapers published in Hong Kong (Kane, 2006). See also Chapter 1's discussion of the varieties of Chinese.

4. In China there is concern that writing via such electronic means is leading people to forget how to write characters by hand, a phenomenon known as character amnesia (提笔忘字 *tíbǐwàngzì*). I see this as a separate issue from non-native speakers learning Chinese as a second/foreign language. See Almog (2019) for a discussion and critique of the arguments around character amnesia.

5. MacKenzie (2018) also argues tones and homophones will prevent Chinese becoming a spoken global lingua franca but this is not the focus of this chapter.

6. Of course not all students in these countries will finish their education able to read and write these characters proficiently but they will nevertheless have some familiarity with the script.

7. Kirkpatrick (2010) makes this point in his discussion of the prospects of Chinese becoming a working language of the Association of Southeast

Asian Nations (ASEAN), but it is equally relevant to my discussion of Chinese as a potential global language.

REFERENCES

Almog, G. (2019). Getting out of hand? Examining the discourse of 'character amnesia'. *Modern Asian Studies, 53*(2), 690–717.

Araya, J. A. (2012, May 21). Mandarin? No, thanks. *The Harvard Crimson.* Retrieved 29 January, 2019, from https://www.thecrimson.com/article/2012/5/21/harvard-mandarin-not-language-of-the-future/

Brock, A. (2014, December 13). Will Chinese replace English as the global language? *Voice of America Learning English.* Retrieved 28 November, 2018, from https://learningenglish.voanews.com/a/will-chinese-replace-english-as-international-language/2554910.html

Bruthiaux, P. (2002). Predicting challenges to English as a global language in the 21st century. *Language Problems & Language Planning, 26*(2), 129–157.

Canagarajah, A.S. (1999). Interrogating the "native speaker fallacy": Non-linguistic roots, non-pedagogical results. In G. Braine (Ed.), *Non-native educators in English language teaching* (pp. 77–92). Lawrence Erlbaum Associates.

Chen, P. (1999). *Modern Chinese: History and sociolinguistics.* Cambridge University Press.

Chen, P. (2001). Functions of phonetic writing in Chinese. In N. Gottlieb & P. Chen (Eds.), *Language planning and language policy: East Asian perspectives* (pp. 75–94). Curzon Press.

Chen, P. (2007). China. In A. Simpson (Ed.), *Language and national identity in Asia* (pp. 141–167). Oxford University Press.

Clements, R. (2019). Brush talk as the 'lingua franca' of diplomacy in Japanese–Korean encounters, c.1600–1868. *The Historical Journal, 62*(2), 289–309.

Cook, V. (1999). Going beyond the native speaker in language teaching. *TESOL Quarterly, 33*(2), 185–209.

Crystal, D. (2003). *English as a global language* (2nd ed.). Cambridge University Press.

Crystal, D. (2012). A global language. In P. Seargeant & J. Swann (Eds.), *English in the world: History, diversity, change* (pp. 151–196). Routledge and The Open University.

DeFrancis, J. (1950). *Nationalism and language reform in China.* Princeton University Press.

DeFrancis, J. (2006). The prospects for Chinese writing reform. *Sino-Platonic Papers, 171,* 1–29.

Denecke, W. (2014). Worlds without translation: Premodern East Asia and the power of character scripts. In S. Bermann & C. Porter (Eds.), *A companion to translation studies* (pp. 204 − 216). Wiley-Blackwell.

Dobrovolsky, M. (2011). Writing and language. In W. O'Grady, J. Archibald & F. Katamba (Eds.), *Contemporary linguistics: An introduction* (2nd ed.) (pp. 523–546). Pearson Education.

Dorren, G. (2018). *Babel: Around the world in twenty languages.* Profile Books.

Education First. (2020). *EF English Proficiency Index 2020.* Retrieved 31 December, 2020, from https://www.ef.com/assetscdn/WIBIwq6RdJvcD9b c8RMd/legacy/__/~/media/centralefcom/epi/downloads/full-reports/ v10/ef-epi-2020-english.pdf

Edwards, J. (2012). *Multilingualism: Understanding linguistic diversity.* Continuum.

Fishman, J.A. (2000). The new linguistic order. In P. O'Meara, H. D. Mehlinger & M. Krain (Eds.), *Globalization and the challenges of a new century: A reader* (pp. 435–442). Indiana University Press.

Fromkin, V., Rodman, R., Hymas, N., Amberber, M., Cox, F., & Thorton, R. (2018). *An introduction to language* (Australia and New Zealand 9th ed.). Cengage Learning Australia.

Galloway, N., & Rose, H. (2015). *Introducing global Englishes.* Routledge.

Gottlieb, N. (2001). Language planning and policy in Japan. In N. Gottlieb & P. Chen (Eds.), *Language planning and language policy: East Asian perspectives* (pp. 21–48). Curzon Press.

Gottlieb, N. (2012). *Language policy in Japan: The challenge of change.* Cambridge University Press.

Gottlieb, N., & Chen, P. (2001). Language planning and language policy in East Asia: An overview. In N. Gottlieb & P. Chen (Eds.), *Language planning and language policy: East Asian perspectives* (pp. 1–20). Curzon Press.

Guo, Y. (2004). *Cultural nationalism in contemporary China: The search for national identity under reform.* Routledge Curzon.

Kan, Q., Owen, N., & Bax, S. (2018). Researching mobile-assisted Chinese-character learning strategies among adult distance learners. *Innovation in Language Learning and Teaching, 12*(1), 56–71.

Kane, D. (2006). *The Chinese language: Its history and current usage.* Tuttle.

King, R. (2007). North and South Korea. In A. Simpson (Ed.), *Language and national identity in Asia* (pp. 200–234). Oxford University Press.

Kirkpatrick, A. (2010). *English as a lingua franca in ASEAN: A multilingual model.* Hong Kong University Press.

Kornicki, P. F. (2018). *Languages, scripts, and Chinese texts in East Asia.* Oxford University Press.

118   J. GIL

Kuo, G. (2011, February 21). Taiwan's literacy rate hits record high. *Taiwan Today*. Retrieved 28 February, 2019, from https://taiwantoday.tw/news.php?unit=10&post=17666

Lane Greene, R. (2012, March/April). Which is the best language to learn? *The Economist 1843 Magazine*. Retrieved 29 January, 2019, from https://www.1843magazine.com/content/ideas/robert-lane-greene/which-best-language-learn

Levy, M., & Steel, C. (2015). Language learner perspectives on the functionality and use of electronic language dictionaries. *ReCall, 27*(2), 177–196.

Lo Bianco, J. (2001). Viet Nam: *Quoc Ngu*, colonialism and language policy. In N. Gottlieb & P. Chen (Eds.), *Language planning and language policy: East Asian perspectives* (pp. 159–206). Curzon Press.

Lu, D. (2008). Pre-imperial Chinese: Its hurdles towards becoming a world language. *Journal of Asian Pacific Communication, 18*(2), 268–279.

MacKenzie, I. (2018). *Language contact and the future of English*. Routledge.

Martinez, A. (2015, January 5). Why we won't all be speaking Mandarin. *Policy Options*. Retrieved 29 January, 2019, http://policyoptions.irpp.org/magazines/environmental-faith/martinez/

McWhorter, J. (2015, January 2). What the world will speak in 2115. *The Wall Street Journal*. Retrieved 21 August, 2015, from http://www.wsj.com/articles/what-the-world-will-speak-in-2115-1420234648

Moser, D. (1991). Why Chinese is so damn hard. *Sino-Platonic Papers, 27*, 59–70.

Moser, D. (2016). *A billion voices: China's search for a common language*. Penguin Books.

Mufwene, S. S. (2013). Globalization, global English, and world English(es): Myths and facts. In N. Coupland (Ed.), *The handbook of language and globalization* (pp. 32–55). Wiley-Blackwell.

Noack, R. (2015, September 24). The future of language. *Washington Post*. Retrieved 28 November, 2018, from https://www.washingtonpost.com/news/worldviews/wp/2015/09/24/the-future-of-language/?noredirect=on&utm_term=.4ace5495f2b7

Norman, J. (1988). *Chinese*. Cambridge University Press.

Phillipson, R. (1992). *Linguistic imperialism*. Oxford University Press.

Premaratne, D. D. (2012). Reforming Chinese characters in the PRC and Japan: New directions in the twenty-first century. *Current Issues in Language Planning, 13*(4), 305–319.

Pullum, G. (2016, January 20). The awful Chinese writing system. *Lingua Franca*. Retrieved 16 May, 2018, from https://www.chronicle.com/blogs/linguafranca/2016/01/20/the-awful-chinese-writing-system

Ramsey, S. R. (1987). *The languages of China*. Princeton University Press.

Rohsenow, J. S. (2004). Fifty years of script and written language reform in the P.R.C.: The genesis of the Language Law of 2001. In M. Zhou & H. Sun (Eds.), *Language policy in the People's Republic of China: Theory and practice since 1949* (pp. 21–43). Kluwer Academic Publishers.

Shei, C., & Hsieh, H. P. (2012). Linkit: A CALL system for learning Chinese characters, words, and phrases. *Computer Assisted Language Learning, 25*(4), 319–338.

Snow, D. (2010). Diglossia in East Asia. *Journal of Asian Pacific Communication, 20*(1), 124–151.

Song, J. J. (2001). North and South Korea: Language policies of divergence and convergence. In N. Gottlieb & P. Chen (Eds.), *Language planning and language policy: East Asian perspectives* (pp. 129–157). Curzon Press.

Taylor, I., & Taylor, M. M. (2014). *Writing and literacy in Chinese, Korean and Japanese* (Revised ed.). John Benjamins.

World Bank. (2019). *Literacy rate, adult total (% of people ages 15 and above).* Retrieved 28 February, 2019, from https://data.worldbank.org/indicator/SE.ADT.LITR.ZS?locations=CN

Zhao, S. (2005). Chinese character modernisation in the digital era: A historical perspective. *Current Issues in Language Planning, 6*(3), 315–378.

Zhao, S. (2010). Flows of technology: Mandarin in cyberspace. In V. Vaish (Ed.), *Globalization of language and culture in Asia: The impact of globalization processes on language* (pp. 139–160). Continuum.

Zhao, S., & Baldauf, R. B. Jr. (2011). Simplifying Chinese characters: Not a simple matter. In J. Fishman & O. García (Eds.), *Handbook of language and ethnic identity volume 2: The success-failure continuum in language and ethnic identity efforts* (pp. 168–179). Oxford University Press.

Zhao, S., & Baldauf, R. B., Jr. (2012). Individual agency in language planning: Chinese script reform as a case study. *Language Problems & Language Planning, 36*(1), 1–24.

CHAPTER 7

Continuation, Coexistence or Replacement?

Abstract Whether Chinese establishes a language comprehensive competitiveness profile sufficient to make it a global language will depend on the outcome of China's rise. This chapter presents three possible scenarios—continuation, in which English remains a global language; coexistence, in which English and Chinese are both global languages; and replacement, in which Chinese becomes a global language instead of English—and discusses how they connect to the possible outcomes of China's rise.

Keywords China's rise · Chinese · Future of Chinese as a global language · Future of English as a global language · Global language

7.1 INTRODUCTION

The previous chapters established the current language comprehensive competitiveness profile of Chinese and demonstrated why a character-based writing system will not prevent it from becoming a global language. The question remains whether, in future, Chinese will have a language comprehensive competitiveness profile sufficient to give it the "special role that is recognized in every country" (Crystal, 2003, p. 3) required of a global language.[1]

© The Author(s), under exclusive license to Springer Nature   121
Switzerland AG 2021
J. Gil, *The Rise of Chinese as a Global Language*,
https://doi.org/10.1007/978-3-030-76171-4_7

In this chapter, I argue this will depend on the outcome of China's rise. To do this, I first summarise the main strands of thought in the literature on China's future, which are: (i) China as a superpower; (ii) China as a major power; (iii) China as a threat; and (iv) China as a declining power. I then present three scenarios for the global future of Chinese and English, and discuss how they connect to these possible outcomes. These scenarios are: (i) continuation, in which English remains a global language; (ii) coexistence, in which English and Chinese are both global languages and (iii) replacement, in which Chinese becomes a global language instead of English. I argue that continuation will result from either China's decline or China as a threat, while coexistence will result from China as a major power, and replacement will result from either China as a superpower or China as a threat.[2]

7.2   THE POSSIBLE OUTCOMES OF CHINA'S RISE

In Chapter 2, I showed that China's rise is a punctuation which will reconfigure the global language system. However, the outcome of China's rise is by no means certain. A review of the literature on this issue suggests four possible outcomes. The first of these is China as a superpower. According to proponents of this view, China will become the world's most powerful country, akin to the USA today. The second is China as a major power. Scholars associated with this view hypothesise China will be a powerful and important country but will not dominate the world. The third is China as a threat. This is the view that China's rise endangers the current international system and a confrontation will occur between China and the USA and its allies. The fourth possible outcome is China's decline, and those who subscribe to this view argue that the array of problems China faces will overwhelm it, and its development will go backwards.

The proceeding review of each of these possible outcomes is not intended to be an exhaustive survey of the literature, which is already vast and growing constantly. Instead, it gives a summary of the main predictions regarding China's rise.

7.2.1   Superpower

Jacques (2009) argues that China will become the most powerful country in the world by the middle of the twenty-first century, and will have at least as much impact on the world as the USA has had over the last 100 years or so. He bases this argument on two factors. Firstly, China's economic and demographic size are far greater than any other country, and as a result, other countries will become increasingly dependent on China. Secondly, China's need for resources will bring more and more countries into relationships with China. China will therefore have a "gravitational pull on every other nation" (p. 431), and will be able to make its relations with them operate in ways that facilitate its interests and goals.

White (2017) similarly argues that China already possesses considerable economic, military and diplomatic power, and with China's economy set to become the largest in the world, it will have the means to further develop and enhance its power. This in turn allows China to impose costs (such as trade sanctions) on other countries for acting in ways it does not like. This constrains their choices and encourages them to accommodate what China wants (White, 2017).

Both Jacques (2009) and White (2017) say China desires to regain its status as a great power and this will require some changes to the international system. Its power will allow it to bring about such changes and gain the support, or at least acquiescence, of other countries in the ways just described. Working in China's favour is that its economic success, based on a combination of rapid economic development and political control, could be seen as an attractive alternative to the Western model of development based on liberal democracy and free market values. The international system may then reflect China's model more than the Western one. This would obviously make it easier for China to pursue its goals (Halper, 2012). According to White (2017), a major war would be required to prevent China becoming the most powerful country in the world.

7.2.2   Major Power

Others see China as important and powerful, but unlikely to ever dominate the world. Within this strand there are those who focus on characteristics of China and those who focus on characteristics of the world as a whole to support their view. Looking at China, some scholars have acknowledged China possesses considerable power resources but have also identified constraints on its influence over other countries and events. Firstly, China lacks close friends and allies to help it pursue its goals, and this limits what it is able to accomplish. Secondly, China has yet to develop a defined and workable idea of what role it wants to play and how it wants to use its power in the world. Related to this, it has not demonstrated the willingness and capacity to lead on global issues. The main focus of China's diplomacy is trade, and it engages with efforts to deal with global issues only when they serve its own interests. Militarily, China is a regional, rather than global power, and lacks the capability to project military power globally. Even in the economic domain there are limits to China's power and influence. It exports mainly low end consumer goods and its products and companies largely lack global brand recognition. Neither is it a leader in science, technology, popular culture or education, and its political system may well constrain it producing the innovation necessary to become one. China also faces serious domestic problems in a range of domains from the political to the social, that occupy much of its attention and resources which then cannot be used for global purposes. Finally, China is constrained in global politics by other countries, especially the USA, as well as established international organisations (Beeson & Li, 2014; Fenby, 2017; Gurtov, 2013; Shambaugh, 2014).

Taking a broader perspective, Brooks (2019) argues that the world has changed in ways which set limits on the extent of China's rise. First of all, there is a very significant technological gap between China and the USA. While China is making progress, this gap is too big to close quickly, meaning China will have a lower level of technology than the USA for decades to come. Secondly, the most advanced military technology in today's world, such as combat aircraft, military satellites and nuclear attack submarines, are more complex than past military technologies and require highly trained personnel to operate them. Developing these technologies and the ability to use them therefore takes time. In addition, their complexity means China cannot produce them by itself and would have to rely on others for materials and expertise. This gives other countries the ability to deny China access, and prevent it from obtaining the most advanced military technologies available. A fourth barrier to superpower status is that the USA's military advantage over China is much bigger than those which existed between rising and established powers in the past. This includes command of the sea, space and air, and the means to command them. Finally, China's population is aging much faster than those of other countries. This reduces its working age population, which will likely slow down economic development. Caring for the aging population will also take resources away from other areas (Brooks, 2019). All of these factors will prevent China from attaining superpower status and being able to dominate the world in the way the USA currently does.

Similarly, Kupchan (2012) argues that although power is diffusing away from the USA (and the West more broadly), its rise to superpower status was a unique event and will not be repeated by another country. Instead, he envisions a world with many rising powers, each with its own political system and each following its own path to development and modernisation. Each rising power will attempt to change the international system to suit its own interests, goals and values. China is one of these, and its economic and political standing make it the leading rising power with the greatest capacity to change the international system. However, others such as India, Brazil, Russia and the Gulf states are doing the same, creating a world of multiple political systems and developmental paths. There will consequently be no one globally dominant country because these various political systems and developmental paths will compete with each other for status and influence. In other words, there will be no model all countries will converge on. Ultimately, whether because of characteristics of the country itself, the world as a whole or a combination of both, proponents of this view believe China will remain a major power.

7.2.3 Threat

The idea that China's rise is a threat first appeared in the mid-1990s and continues to be advanced today. Scholars such as Allison (2017), Bernstein and Munro (1997), Gertz (2002), Huntington (1996), Kagan (2008) and Mearsheimer (2001, 2006, 2010) have argued that China's burgeoning power and influence will disrupt the international system and have a variety of negative consequences. The threat posed by China is said to be ideological, economic and military.

From the perspective of ideology, subscribers to the China threat view point out that China has a very different political system from the USA and other Western countries, and may seek to export this system to the rest of the world. China's economic activities are also considered a threat for several reasons. Firstly, the trade deficits many countries have with China harm their economies. Secondly, China engages in unfair trading practices like protecting its own markets, restricting foreign access to its markets, undervaluing its currency and demanding transfer of technology as a condition of foreign companies operating in China. The size and importance of China's economy also mean China can use access to its markets as a diplomatic tool to get what it wants from other countries. China is seen as a military threat because its economic power gives it the ability to develop its military forces. China's defence spending has increased considerably since the 1990s, and those who see China's rise as a threat fear its armed forces will one day be strong enough to challenge and even defeat those of the USA (Broomfield, 2003; Deng, 2008).

A variation of the China as a threat view sees China's weaknesses, rather than its strengths, as a danger to the international system. Shirk (2008), for example, describes China as a "fragile superpower" (p. 6). By this she means that although China appears strong on the global stage, it is beset by a number of domestic problems which influence how it behaves and limit its ability to cooperate with other countries. Ensuring economic development continues, pursuing reunification with Taiwan and standing up for China's interests in relations with the USA and Japan determine the legitimacy of the CCP, and therefore take precedence over the concerns of the international community. This means the Chinese government will act to protect itself, even if it comes at the cost of a confrontation with another country. Whether due to strength or weakness, China's rise will consequently create tensions and confrontations should this outcome eventuate.[3]

7.2.4   Decline

Other scholars believe that China's rise will fail, and the country will experience a serious deterioration in its power and influence. The most well-known expression of this view is Gordon G. Chang's (2001) prediction that China's political, economic, environmental and social problems had become so serious that the CCP government would collapse within five years and the country would experience a period of turmoil.

Less dramatic versions of the decline strand in the literature on China's future see its development stalling. China's remarkable economic development, as mentioned above, has been based largely on the cheap production of exports, but this cannot continue indefinitely, and the focus of the economy will need to shift if China is to become a superpower. Pei (2006, 2008) argues that China's political system is not capable of undertaking this transformation. He says China is in a "trapped transition" (2008, p. 9) where economic and political reform have not been extensive enough. The political system functions to maintain the power and privilege of the elite, rather than the development of the whole of society, and this creates corruption and inequalities. Under such circumstances, China will be less able to provide essential services such as health care, law enforcement and education to its citizens, and will experience a long period of stagnation. This will in turn mean China will not be able to meaningfully contribute to, let alone lead, efforts to address global challenges. For scholars in this camp, China is a declining power.

7.3 THREE SCENARIOS FOR THE GLOBAL FUTURE OF CHINESE AND ENGLISH

The possible outcomes of China's rise will have different implications for the position of Chinese and English in the global language system. But how can we say what the future of Chinese and English will be without knowing which of these possible outcomes will eventuate? The best way of dealing with the inherit difficulties of making predictions about the future is to consider different scenarios. According to Cooper and Layard (2002), scenarios are "alternative futures within a given domain" (p. 7). In the remainder of this chapter, I develop three scenarios for the future of Chinese and English as global languages, namely the continuation of English as a global language, the coexistence of English and Chinese as global languages and the replacement of English as a global language by Chinese.

Cooper and Layard (2002) further specify that each scenario must be plausible—even if unlikely—and this requires them to be based on what is happening in the present or what has been observed in another domain and could apply to the domain under consideration. To ensure this, I connect my scenarios to the possible outcomes of China's rise discussed above. I also draw on recent developments relevant to the macroacquisition of Chinese and English, as well as past examples of the macroacquisition of other languages. I then use this information to explain whether and how it would be possible for Chinese to obtain the required features of a global language.

7.3.1 Continuation: English Remains a Global Language

Continuation will result from decline or threat. To begin with decline, geostrategic and economic competitiveness are two of the main drivers of macroacquisition, so if China's development stagnates or goes backwards, people will be far less interested in learning Chinese. Japanese language learning followed a similar pattern. In the 1980s and 1990s, Japanese language learning was very popular due to Japan's surging economy and growing influence in the world, but the number of learners fell sharply at both school and university level following Japan's long period of economic trouble (de Kretser & Spence-Brown, 2010; Lo Bianco, 2009; McGee et al., 2013).[4] The only other component of language comprehensive competitiveness to provide strong support for the macroacquisition of Chinese is population competitiveness. The remaining components—policy competitiveness, cultural competitiveness, script competitiveness, scientific/technological competitiveness and educational competitiveness—only offer medium or weak support for macroacquisition. It is therefore unlikely these will be enough to make Chinese a global language in the absence of geostrategic and economic competitiveness.

Alternatively, if China is a threat, or is perceived as one, it is likely to create resistance to learning Chinese and to the idea of Chinese as a global language. In particular, its association with the PRC and its Communist government could do this. Anders Corr (2018), publisher of the *Journal of Political Risk*, called for a boycott of Putonghua, describing it as "a medium for authoritarian influence from a political party that some compare to dictatorship, totalitarianism and fascism", and "a tool of CCP power". This has obvious implications for macroacquisition—if people do not accept Chinese because of these associations, they will be reluctant to learn it and use it in their lives.

More broadly, the presence of Chinese in education systems may be reduced if China is seen as a threat. For example, a draft of India's National Education Policy included Mandarin on the list of languages which could be taught in schools, but it was removed from the final version due to security concerns raised during the consultation process with the Ministry of Human Resource Development and Ministry of External Affairs (Jebaraj & Haidar, 2020).[5] These security concerns were not specified, but this does show Chinese language learning can be affected when China is perceived as a threat.

Similarly, opportunities for in-country language learning experience may be curtailed. The Australian government issued a travel warning for China following the announcement of the Hong Kong National Security Law,[6] advising Australians they risked arbitrary detention (Dziedzic, 2020). Travel warnings mean schools and universities cannot arrange in-country experiences such as study tours, and this can affect numbers of language learners. This happened with Indonesian language learning in Australia after the terrorist attacks in Indonesia in the early 2000s

(Firdaus, 2013). It is likely such things would happen more widely if the outcome of China's rise eventuated in a real or perceived threat.

This does not mean that there would be no Chinese language learning. Chinese would still be learned by military and intelligence services personnel for security reasons. An example can again be found in India, where tensions over the border with China have increased in recent years. The Ministry of Home Affairs stated that members of the Indo-Tibet Border Police (ITBP) should learn both spoken and written Mandarin to better communicate with and understand the tactics of their Chinese counterparts (Ranjan, 2020). However, this obviously does not encourage macroacquisition by actors outside of the military and intelligence services.

These developments confirm Ferguson's (2012) argument that there must be "an absence of ideological resistance" (p. 477) for a language to be widely acquired as a second/additional language and adopted for various purposes.

In the case of both decline and threat, Chinese would not have a language comprehensive competitiveness profile as strong as the one English does. Chinese would not expand its standing as an official language or a priority foreign language, and the latter would recede. It would retain its current significant standing as a native language, but this is only one component of the special role of a global language. English would remain a global language.

7.3.2 Coexistence: English and Chinese as Global Languages

This scenario will eventuate if China's rise results in the country becoming a major power. In such circumstances, Chinese would not displace English as a global language but its use and status would increase. As mentioned in Chapter 1, there are already ample examples of Chinese occupying more physical and virtual space.[7] Here I provide some additional examples from Adelaide's central business district (CBD), where in recent years the use of Chinese has become more prominent and expanded into more areas. These examples include shop signs, advertisements and posters.

Many of these signs are intended to bring Chinese customers into the businesses which display them. The sign in Fig. 7.1 hangs prominently at the entrance to a pharmacist in a shopping plaza in Rundle Mall, Adelaide's main shopping mall. The text says, "Welcome, we speak

Fig. 7.1   Terry White Chemist, Coles Rundle Place Mall

Chinese". It is clearly intended for a Chinese-speaking audience as there is no English equivalent provided on the sign.

Similarly, an advertisement on tables of the food court in the same shopping plaza (Fig. 7.2) encourages Chinese customers to explore the range of shopping opportunities available in the plaza and directs them to WeChat for further information. The text reads, "Don't miss any surprises. Visit our official WeChat account". This connects physical and virtual uses of Chinese. Again, it is aimed at a Chinese-speaking audience with no English in the sign. It also has the Rundle Place name and logo, suggesting it was created by the management of the plaza.

Another business, the Unique Opal Mine shop in Rundle Mall, also uses Chinese in its sign (Fig. 7.3). The text reads, "This shop supplies a large quantity of opals, (you're) welcome to come and to buy and inquire". In this sign the Chinese text appears alongside English text, but conveys a different message, focused on purchasing opals rather than the model opal mine.

Fig. 7.2 Table top signs, Rundle Plaza Food Court

Fig. 7.3 Opal Shop Rundle Mall

The sign in Fig. 7.4, outside a luggage shop in Rundle Mall, reads "(this shop) sells luggage". There is again English text on the sign, but while the English text emphasises a current sale, the Chinese text informs readers of what products the shop sells.

Another sign, at the entrance to Central Market, provides an overview of the city's attractions and basic directions in Chinese along with English equivalents (Fig. 7.5). It also has a QR code to link to UWAI. It too is aimed at a Chinese-speaking audience who would like to use Chinese for navigating the city. It has the Adelaide City Council logo in the bottom right corner, making it an official sign.

These signs in Adelaide's CBD were created by a variety of actors, from the city council to private businesses. All of them share a perception of Chinese as a language of economic opportunity, and a perception of China as important for the city's economy. Through them Chinese speakers can experience shopping and other attractions in Chinese, much like English speakers can use English in a variety of contexts around

Fig. 7.4 Bag Heaven Store Gawler Place Rundle Mall

Fig. 7.5 Central Market entrance

the world. The interesting point about these examples is that prior to 2016, Chinese was used only in the city's Chinatown and not anywhere else. Following Hult's (2009) approach to languages in public space, such signs reflect the growing niche of Chinese in the global ecology of languages. They can be seen to constitute a developing "parallel space" for Chinese. The examples mentioned elsewhere in this book indicate Chinese is used in similar ways in other cities in various parts of the world.

Chinese has been adopted for such purposes because of the presence of Chinese speakers around the world. This highlights the status of Chinese as a native language in diaspora communities as discussed elsewhere in this book. Such uses of Chinese give it some of the uses of an official language, even if it is not granted this status. The need or desire to use Chinese in these ways is also likely to add to its standing as a priority foreign language. However, this would not be enough to displace English as a global language.

7.3.3 Replacement: Chinese as a Global Language

The third scenario is replacement. English is well-established as a global language primarily because the USA has been and remains the world leader across the components of language comprehensive competitiveness. It was also able to use its power and influence to shape the international system, especially following World War II. This included the establishment of important international organisations like the United Nations (UN) and the International Monetary Fund (IMF), and sponsorship of re-development through the Marshall Plan (Graddol, 1997). The replacement of English as a global language by Chinese will therefore most obviously result from China becoming a superpower.

If this occurred, China would similarly be the world leader across the components of language comprehensive competitiveness and be able to shape the international system. China is attempting to position itself as a leader on global issues such as free trade, globalisation, climate change and space exploration. This is another similarity to English, which was helped in becoming a global language by its association with the inventions of the Industrial Revolution and developments in science and technology in the USA (Crystal, 2003). One notable Chinese phenomenon regarding shaping the international system is the Belt and Road Initiative (BRI), which is about connecting China to the rest of the world through roads, railways and ports, and involves substantial amounts of investment across the world. If China's initiatives are successful, Chinese will be the language associated with new developments and ideas, greatly encouraging its macroacquisition.

How will this lead to Chinese having the special role required for global language status? Most obviously, its standing as a priority foreign language will increase. This could then provide a platform for the expansion of the native language and official language roles. Expansion of the foreign language role will obviously add to the number of speakers of Chinese. Of course, this does not in itself produce native speakers—or even speakers with native-like proficiency in most cases—but the expansion of Chinese as a foreign language could indirectly increase the number of native speakers. Crystal (2006) points out that many people who have learned English as a foreign language speak it to their children in the home so they can acquire it as a native language. The same could also happen with Chinese as proficiency in the language is perceived as important or essential in a world in which China is the superpower.

As for the official language role, academics, journalists and government officials in various countries have argued that granting English official status will improve a country's ability to interact with the rest of the world and facilitate the population's learning of the language. Should Chinese become a priority foreign language due to China's superpower status, some countries may decide to make it an official or co-official language for these same reasons. This would obviously increase the number of countries in which Chinese has official status, and could also result in Chinese being used in government, law courts, broadcasting and the press. In 2018, Pakistan made Chinese an official language (along with English, Urdu and Arabic), so this is possible (ANI, 2018).

It should be acknowledged that many have argued that English will remain a global language even if another country becomes a superpower instead of the USA (see, for example, Bruthiaux, 2002; Montgomery, 2013; MacKenzie, 2018). They argue English is now so widespread, widely used and accepted as a global language that it will retain this status regardless of changes in global politics. However, Ostler (2010) has challenged this view, arguing that as non-English-speaking countries become more powerful and influential, they will want their languages used more in global interactions and will not necessarily remain content to use English. As he says, the argument that English will remain a global language in such circumstances is "predicated on a belief that an unprecedented, and strangely cringing, deference will be assumed by newly dominant countries – and indeed majority speech communities – and that this attitude will continue indefinitely, even as the pioneering glories of the English-speaking nations recede into the past" (p. 270).

As I've argued elsewhere, China's government and people see their country's rise as regaining its lost position as a superpower. There have also long been tensions and concerns over the impact of English on Chinese culture and identity (Gil, 2016). A superpower China is therefore likely to advocate greater use of Chinese rather than accept English as a global language forever.

Replacement could also result from the threat outcome of China's rise. If China won a confrontation with the USA and its allies, it would also be in a position to establish a new international system, and possibly even to incorporate other countries into its political, economic and social system. Chinese would again be the language most associated with this new international system. China may also seek to implement policies for greater use of Chinese as part of this process. However, at least some degree of resistance to Chinese as a global language would accompany this scenario.

A parallel can be drawn here with Russian, the lingua franca of the former Soviet Union. From the 1930s, Soviet policy focused on russification through the use of the Cyrillic alphabet for writing systems of all languages, standardisation of languages based on Russian grammar, the requirement to use Russian in all aspects of life and compulsory Russian language study in schools (Pavlenko, 2006, 2008).[8] Russian was intended to unify the republics and serve as a symbol of Soviet culture and people. It was also the dominant language of the military, politics, science, education, literature and administration, and this encouraged its acquisition and use, even to the point that it became a first language for some. Consequently, other languages were relegated to lower status and restricted use, and this met with resistance and resentment, especially in countries which were forcibly incorporated into the Soviet Union (Kellner-Heinkele & Landau, 2012; Schlyter, 2003).

The Soviet Union also extended its control over Eastern and Central Europe, essentially making them part of the Soviet order. Here too Russian became a compulsory language and in some cases encountered resistance. In Hungary, for example, many people intentionally did not learn Russian to demonstrate resistance towards the Soviet government. In Bruen and Sheridan's (2016) words, "not learning Russian reached the level of being a national sport" (p. 153).

Language became a focal point of mass demonstrations and protests in the final years of the Soviet Union. In some republics, steps were also taken to remove Russian from street names, public signs and billboards. When the Soviet Union collapsed, many successor states embarked on de-russification programs, although to different extents and with different results. Eastern and Central European countries also replaced Russian language education with English to a large degree (Brown, 2013; Bruen & Sheridan, 2016; Kellner-Heinkele & Landau, 2012; Pavlenko, 2006, 2008).

If replacement came about via the threat outcome of China's rise, Chinese would increase its standing as an official and priority foreign language, and to a lesser extent as a native language, based on the Russian example discussed above. However, Chinese would be a fragile global language and be so only as long as China was able to hold the system together. Like Russian, its position would be resisted, and ultimately wound back if the system collapsed.

Some signs of resistance to Chinese can already be seen in Hong Kong, which has come under increasing control by the mainland government. Together with an influx of mainland migrants and visitors, the use of Mandarin has expanded considerably. In 1997, when China resumed sovereignty, only around one around quarter of the population spoke Mandarin. Today, more than half of the population speak it (Liu, 2017; Tam, 2016). Mandarin, and specifically Putonghua, is seen as a threat to the linguistic and cultural identity of Hong Kong. The preservation of Cantonese was an issue in the Umbrella Revolution of 2014 (Tam, 2016), and was again used as a symbol of resistance to the mainland government and its policies throughout the protests of 2019 to 2020. Again, ideological resistance could count heavily against Chinese becoming a global language, even if China was to dominate the international system.

7.4   CONCLUSION

In her analysis of the rise and decline of lingua francas, Wright (2016) says that "there is often a critical point where the advantage to the individual of acquiring a different lingua franca becomes clear and it eclipses the old" (p. 133). There has been much academic and popular speculation as to whether, and when, this point might arrive for English and Chinese. In this chapter, I approached this question through an examination of the possible outcomes of China's rise and mapped these onto scenarios for the future of Chinese and English. This analysis shows that the continuation of English as a global language, the coexistence of English and Chinese as global languages and the replacement of English as a global language by Chinese are all possible.

In the short term future, continuation is the most likely scenario. This is because China is not yet a superpower and may not be able to overcome the obstacles to becoming one. Chinese will not have the necessary language comprehensive competitiveness profile to encourage macroacquisition enough for it to obtain the characteristics of a global language. In addition, at the time of writing, there are growing tensions between China and other countries that are creating some resistance to the macroacquisition of Chinese.

China is nevertheless a major power already, and the use of Chinese is increasing as described in this book. The "parallel space" where Chinese is used is not displacing English but does nevertheless show Chinese is being used more, and will likely continue to expand. In the medium term future then, coexistence is likely to eventuate.

Replacement is possible only in the long term future. It would require China to overcome all of its current problems and challenges, and establish itself as a world leader in the important spaces and roles that were once solely associated with the USA, or at least Western countries more broadly, and English. This would give Chinese the language comprehensive competitiveness profile needed for macroacquisition to occur sufficiently for it to have the characteristics of a global language, but it is not likely to happen quickly.

NOTES

1. As discussed in Chapter 1, this special role has three components: native language, official language and foreign language.
2. I first articulated the basic idea and argument of this chapter in my opinion piece Gil, J. (2019, March 25). Will Mandarin be the next global language? *Asia Times* (https://www.asiatimes.com/2019/03/opinion/will-mandarin-be-the-next-global-language/). Here I present a significantly expanded and more detailed version.
3. Here I use the term confrontation in the broad sense of competition across a number of areas, not just military conflict.
4. This is not the only reason for the decrease in the number of students taking Japanese. These studies show that policy changes, lack of resources,

the perceived difficulty of Japanese and curriculum and timetabling issues also contributed to this situation.

5. The text of the document states, "In addition to high quality offerings in Indian languages and English, foreign languages, such as Korean, Japanese, Thai, French, German, Spanish, Portuguese, and Russian, will also be offered at the secondary level". It should be noted that India's Higher Education Secretary Amit Khare said the languages on the list were intended as examples only, and schools could teach other languages (Jebaraj & Haidar, 2020).

6. The Hong Kong National Security Law is a wide ranging law aimed at preventing secession, subversion, terrorism and collusion with foreign forces. It contains harsh penalties including lengthy prison sentences for these offences. The law is vague, meaning any activity could potentially be considered to be secession, subversion, terrorism or collusion with foreign forces (*ABC News*, 2020; Clift, 2020).

7. Other languages may also increase their use and status. For example, Graddol (1997) argues Chinese, Hindi/Urdu, Spanish and Arabic will be the world's dominant languages alongside English by the middle of the twenty-first century. Here I focus only on Chinese and English.

8. An earlier phase of russification occurred in the tsarist era from the middle of the nineteenth century. The original goal of Soviet policy was to support the use and development of languages other than Russian, and various measures to do so were implemented in the 1920s, before policy shifted away from this goal in the 1930s. In the last years of the Soviet Union there was another shift, back towards supporting other languages (Brown, 2013; Kellner-Heinkele & Landau, 2012; Pavlenko, 2006).

REFERENCES

ABC News. (2020). What's in Hong Kong's new national security law imposed by China, and why is it so controversial? Retrieved 15 October, 2020, from https://www.abc.net.au/news/2020-07-01/what-is-in-hong-kongs-new-china-imposed-national-security-law/12409024

Allison, G. (2017). *Destined for war: Can America and China escape Thucydides's trap?* Houghton Mifflin Harcourt.

ANI. (2018). *Mandarin approved as official language of Pakistan.* Retrieved May 18, 2019, from https://www.aninews.in/news/world/asia/mandarin-approved-as-official-language-of-pakistan201802192310240006/

Beeson, M., & Li, F. (2014). *China's regional relations: Evolving foreign policy dynamics.* Lynne Rienner.

Bernstein, R., & Munro, R. H. (1997). *The coming conflict with China.* Alfred A. Knoff.

Brooks, S. G. (2019). Power transitions, then and now: Five new structural barriers that will constrain China's rise. *China International Strategy Review,* 1(1), 65–83.

Broomfield, E. V. (2003). Perceptions of danger: The China threat theory. *Journal of Contemporary China, 12*(35), 265–284.

Brown, K. D. (2013). Language policy and education: Space and place in multilingual post-Soviet states. *Annual Review of Applied Linguistics, 33,* 238–257.

Bruen, J., & Sheridan, V. (2016). The impact of the collapse of communism and EU accession on language education policy and practice in Central and Eastern Europe: Two case-studies focusing on English and Russian as foreign languages in Hungary and Eastern Germany. *Current Issues in Language Planning, 17*(2), 141–160.

Bruthiaux, P. (2002). Predicting challenges to English as a global language in the 21st century. *Language Problems & Language Planning, 26*(2), 129–157.

Chang, G. G. (2001). *The coming collapse of China.* Random House.

Clift, B. (2020, July 3). Hong Kong activists now face a choice: Say silent, or flee the city. The world must give them a path to safety. *The Conversation.* Retrieved 15 October, 2020, from https://theconversation.com/hong-kong-activists-now-face-a-choice-stay-silent-or-flee-the-city-the-world-must-give-them-a-path-to-safety-141880

Cooper, R. N., & Layard, R. (2002). Introduction. In R. N. Cooper & R. Layard (Eds.), *What the future holds: Insights from social science.* MIT Press.

Crystal, D. (2003). *English as a global language* (2nd ed.). Cambridge University Press.

Crystal, D. (2006). English worldwide. In R. Hogg & D. Denison (Eds.), *A history of the English language* (pp. 420–439). Cambridge University Press.

de Kretser, A., & Spence-Brown, R. (2010). *The current state of Japanese language education in Australian schools.* Education Services Australia.

Deng, Y. (2008). *China's struggle for status: The realignment of international relations.* Cambridge University Press.

Dziedzic, S. (2020, July 7). Australians at risk of arbitrary arrest in China, DFAT travel advice warns. *ABC News.* Retrieved 1 September, 2020, from https://www.abc.net.au/news/2020-07-07/dfat-changes-travel-advice-for-australians-in-china/12431134?utm_source=abc_news&utm_medium=content_shared&utm_content=mail&utm_campaign=abc_news

Fenby, J. (2017). *Will China dominate the 21st century?* (2nd ed.). Polity Press.

Ferguson, G. (2012). English in language policy and management. In B. Spolsky (Ed.), *The Cambridge handbook of language policy* (pp. 475–498). Cambridge University Press.

Firdaus. (2013). Indonesian language education in Australia: Politics, policies and responses. *Asian Studies Review, 37*(1), 24–41.

Gertz, B. (2002). *The China threat: How the People's Republic targets America.* Regnery Publishing Inc.

Gil, J. (2016). English language education policies in the People's Republic of China. In R. Kirkpatrick (Ed.), *English language education policy in Asia* (pp. 49–90). Springer.

Graddol, D. (1997). *The future of English?* The British Council.

Gurtov, M. (2013). *Will this be China's century? A skeptic's view.* Lynne Rienner.

Halper, S. (2012). *The Beijing consensus: Legitimizing authoritarianism in our time.* Basic Books.

Hult, F. M. (2009). Language ecology and linguistic landscape analysis. In E. Shohamy & D. Gorter (Eds.), *Linguistic landscape: Expanding the scenery* (pp. 88–104). Routledge.

Huntington, S. P. (1996). *The clash of civilisations and the remaking of world order.* Simon & Schuster.

Jacques, M. (2009). *When China rules the world: The end of the Western world and the birth of a new global order.* The Penguin Press.

Jebaraj, P., & Haidar, S. (2020, August 1). National Education Policy 2020: Mandarin dropped from language list. *The Hindu.* Retrieved 1 August, 2020, from https://www.thehindu.com/education/national-educat ion-policy-2020-mandarin-dropped-from-language-list/article32249227.ece

Kagan, R. (2008). *The return of history and the end of dreams.* Alfred A. Knopf.

Kellner-Heinkele, B., & Landau, J. M. (2012). *Language politics in contemporary Central Asia: National and ethnic identity and the Soviet legacy.* I.B. Tauris.

Kupchan, C. A. (2012). *No one's world: The West, the rising rest, and the coming global turn.* Oxford University Press.

Liu, J. (2017, June 29). Cantonese v Mandarin: When Hong Kong languages get political. *BBC News.* Retrieved 20 July, 2020, from https://www.bbc. com/news/world-asia-china-40406429

Lo Bianco, J. (2009). Return of the good times? Japanese Teaching Today. *Japanese Studies, 29*(3), 331–336.

MacKenzie, I. (2018). *Language contact and the future of English.* Routledge.

McGee, A., Ashton, K., Dunn, K., & Taniwaki, T. (2013). *Japanese language education in New Zealand: An evaluative literature review of the decline in students since 2005.* Palmerston North: IPC Tertiary Institution. Retrieved 14 August, 2020, from https://mro.massey.ac.nz/handle/10179/14075

Mearsheimer, J. J. (2001). *The tragedy of great power politics.* W.W. Norton.

Mearsheimer, J. J. (2006). China's unpeaceful rise. *Current History, 105*(690), 160–162.

Mearsheimer, J. J. (2010). The gathering storm: China's challenge to US power in Asia. *The Chinese Journal of International Politics, 3*(4), 381–396.

Montgomery, S. L. (2013). *Does science need a global language? English and the future of research.* The University of Chicago Press.

Ostler, N. (2010). *The last lingua franca: English until the return of Babel.* Walker Publishing Company.

Pavlenko, A. (2006). Russian as a lingua franca. *Annual Review of Applied Linguistics, 26,* 78–99.

Pavlenko, A. (2008). Multilingualism in post-Soviet countries: Language revival, language removal, and sociolinguistic theory. *International Journal of Bilingual Education and Bilingualism, 11*(3–4), 275–314.

Pei, M. (2006). The dark side of China's rise. *Foreign Policy, 153,* 32–40.

Pei, M. (2008). *China's trapped transition: The limits of developmental autocracy.* Harvard University Press.

Schlyter, B. N. (2003). Sociolinguistic changes in transformed Central Asian societies. In J. Maurais & M. A. Morris (Eds.), *Languages in a globalising world* (pp. 157–187). Cambridge University Press.

Shambaugh, D. (2014, June 24). *The illusion of Chinese power.* Brooking Institution. Retrieved 21 January, 2018 from https://www.brookings.edu/opinions/the-illusion-of-chinese-power/

Shirk, S. (2008). *China: Fragile superpower.* Oxford University Press.

Ranjan, M. (2020, July 18). Make Mandarin must for troops, ITBP instructed. *The Tribune India.* Retrieved 24 July, 2020, from https://www.tribuneindia.com/news/nation/make-mandarin-must-for-troops-itbp-instructed-114737

Tam, G. (2016, August 3). Tongue-tied in Hong Kong: The fight for two systems and two languages. *Foreign Affairs.* Retrieved 20 July, 2020, from https://www.foreignaffairs.com/articles/china/2016-08-03/tongue-tied-hong-kong

White, H. (2017). Without America: Australia in the new Asia. *Quarterly Essay, 68,* 1–81.

Wright, S. (2016). *Language policy and language planning: From nationalism to globalisation* (2nd ed.). Palgrave Macmillan.

CHAPTER 8

Conclusion

Abstract This book analysed the macroacquisition of Chinese and its implications for the future of English as a global language. It used the conceptual framework of language comprehensive competitiveness and drew on existing data from various sources as well as original data from Chinese language learners, Chinese language teachers and Chinese scholars. This chapter summarises the findings of the book and makes suggestions for further research.

Keywords Chinese · English · Global language · Language comprehensive competitiveness · Macroacquisition

8.1 Introduction

I set out to investigate "Chinese fever", the worldwide interest in Chinese language learning brought about by China's rise. I viewed this phenomenon as an instance of macroacquisition where many actors seek to add Chinese to their linguistic repertoires, and one which would have implications for the global language system. I asked two questions, *What is driving the macroacquisition of Chinese?*, and *What are the implications of the macroacquisition of Chinese for the future of English as a global language?*

In this chapter I summarise the findings of the book and make suggestions for further research.

8.2   WHAT ARE THE ANSWERS TO THE KEY QUESTIONS?

The first question focused on why actors want to add Chinese to their linguistic repertoires. The conceptual framework of language comprehensive competitiveness offered a useful way of analysing this because its components set out the resources which make a language valuable and desirable within the global ecology of languages. I investigated the language comprehensive competitiveness of Chinese from the objective perspective (the current standing, uses and resources available in and through Chinese) and the subjective perspective (people's perceptions, ideas and beliefs about the association of Chinese with various forms of power and resources).

Looking at the macroacquisition of Chinese from the objective perspective, geostrategic, economic and population competitiveness most strongly support it. Policy, cultural, scientific/technological and educational competitiveness also offer some support. Script competitiveness is the component of language comprehensive competitiveness which offers the least support for the macroacquisition of Chinese. From the subjective perspective, geostrategic competitiveness, population competitiveness and economic competitiveness most strongly support the macroacquisition of Chinese. Cultural competitiveness, policy competitiveness and educational competitiveness also offer some support but not as much as those three components, and script competitiveness even less so. Scientific/technological competitiveness offers the least support for the macroacquisition of Chinese in subjective terms.

Overall then, geostrategic, population and economic competitiveness are primarily responsible for the macroacquisition of Chinese. They are the components of language comprehensive competitiveness where the standing, use and resources available in and through Chinese are most obvious. They are also the components which are most salient in the minds of the learners, teachers and scholars who participated in this project.

The second question focused on what the macroacquisition of Chinese means for the future of English as a global language. Laying out and analysing scenarios was a useful way to address this question, and showed that English could remain a global language, coexist with Chinese as a global language or be replaced by Chinese as a global language depending on the outcome of China's rise. Continuation will result from either China's decline or China as a threat, while coexistence will result from China as a major power, and replacement will result from either China as a superpower or China as a threat.

Continuation is most likely in the short term future, given China's current situation. However, there is already some evidence of coexistence, and this is likely to increase in the medium term future. Replacement seems possible only in the long term future, considering the gaps in the current language comprehensive competitiveness profile of Chinese compared to that of English.

Importantly, the character-based written script is not as significant an obstacle to global language status as many have assumed. The common argument that the script will prevent Chinese becoming a global language is founded on flawed assumptions about proficiency, a lack of recognition of the use of technology in the learning and use of characters, unawareness of the historical precedent for the adoption of characters outside of China and an excessive focus on linguistic properties.

8.3   WHERE TO NEXT?

The macroacquisition of Chinese and its implications for the future of English as a global language will be important areas of research in the years ahead. There are several aspects of this topic which require more attention.

Most obviously, further studies should be conducted on Chinese language learners and teachers in a range of countries and at various levels of education. Such studies will deepen our understanding of the reasons driving the macroacquisition of Chinese from the subjective perspective. Both Duff (2006) and Stebbins (2001) have argued that generalisability can be built up through a series or collection of small-scale studies, and this would be an appropriate way forward for studies of the language comprehensive competitiveness of Chinese.

Longitudinal studies which track and analyse changes in the objective and subjective perspectives of the language comprehensive competitiveness of Chinese will also increase our understanding of its macroacquisition and enable us to build a dynamic language comprehensive competitiveness profile. As the examples of Japanese, Indonesian and Russian mentioned earlier in this book show, the situation of a language and the way it is perceived can and does change over time. Establishing if and how this occurs with Chinese will be an important task for researchers. Following Dörnyei (2007), data on the objective and subjective perspectives should be collected at multiple points in time and compared. Again, such longitudinal studies should be conducted across a number of countries and with diverse groups of participants.

It will also be worthwhile for future studies to include participants other than Chinese language learners and Chinese language teachers so as to gain a more complete understanding of the subjective perspective on the language comprehensive competitiveness of Chinese. Such participants could include parents and school/university administrators as they have been shown to have an important influence on language learning (Asia Education Foundation, 2010; Orton, 2008, 2016). This will also allow comparisons to be made between learners', teachers', parents' and administrators' views on why people want to acquire Chinese.

Some scholars have pointed out that more information is needed on the results of Asian language learning, including Chinese (see, for example, Elder et al., 2012; Lo Bianco, 2012; Orton, 2016). In line with this, further studies could also trace the outcomes of Chinese language learning for learners. What levels of proficiency do they achieve? What do they use their Chinese for and does this match the expectations they had when they started learning the language? These questions are particularly pertinent in light of recent online debates about the value of Chinese proficiency for finding a job in China (see, for example, Huang, 2019) and for developing expertise on China (see, for example, Cheng, 2021). The outcomes learners achieve may also influence the subjective perspective of the language comprehensive competitiveness of Chinese.

Another area for further research is comparisons of the language comprehensive competitiveness of Chinese to that of other languages which are, to various extents, also expanding their use and status and receiving greater interest from learners. These include Spanish, Arabic, Korean and Hindi (see, for example, the discussion in Ammon, 2013 and Vaish, 2010). Important questions to explore here include: are the components of language comprehensive competitiveness which drive the macroacquisition of these languages the same as or different from those which drive the macroacquisition of Chinese? What are the reasons for the similarities and differences across the macroacquisition of various languages?

Regarding the implications of the macroacquisition of Chinese for the future of English as a global language, further studies will be able to monitor which outcome of China's rise and which scenario for Chinese and English as global languages eventuates. These studies can provide detailed descriptions of continuation, coexistence or replacement. Given the current state of affairs outlined in Chapter 7, documenting the emerging coexistence of Chinese as a global language should be the focus of such studies. Descriptions and analyses of the use of Chinese in physical and virtual space from around the world will do this. Those researchers interested in pursuing this can turn to linguistic landscape studies for guidance, such as those produced by Lou (2012) and Wang et al. (2016).

Turning to the teaching of Chinese, Chinese language educators and those who research it are often concerned with how to attract more learners into their courses and retain these learners over time. These are complex issues and much effort has been devoted to resolving them (see, for example, Asia Education Foundation, 2010; Orton, 2008, 2016). Understanding the language comprehensive competitiveness profile of Chinese can contribute to these goals. Previous studies have recommended articulating the benefits of Chinese language learning to students, teachers, parents and educational administrators as one important recruitment and retention strategy (Asia Education Foundation, 2010; Orton, 2016; Singh & Han, 2015). The language comprehensive competitiveness profile of Chinese sets out the association of Chinese with various forms of power and resources, and thus provides the information needed to explain how one can benefit from learning Chinese and the domains in which it can be useful. Teachers and researchers can cooperate to develop appropriate and engaging ways of communicating this, such as videos, information sessions, brochures, posters and displays. Such efforts will help schools and universities to, as Singh and Han (2015) advise, "increase the value and valuing of Chinese in their communities" (p. 171).

The language comprehensive competitiveness profile of Chinese can also help identify opportunities for developing and expanding Chinese language education. For example, most of the Chinese language learners who participated in this study did not see Chinese as useful for accessing developments in the fields of science and technology or for pursuing education and research, despite evidence for growth in the scientific/technological and educational competitiveness of Chinese from the objective perspective. Learners may be unaware of the developments in these areas discussed in Chapter 3. Once again, teachers and researchers could devise ways to explain the scientific/technological and educational competitiveness of Chinese to learners—especially those with an existing interest in these fields—and then determine if this has any effect on enrolment and retention. Following on from this, Chinese for Specific Purposes courses could also be developed to enable learners to use Chinese in science and technology and education. This is important for recruitment and retention because previous studies have highlighted the need for courses to be appropriate to learners and their goals (Orton, 2008, 2016; Singh & Han, 2015).

More broadly, as Chinese language learning becomes more popular and the language is used more widely, researchers and practitioners will likely encounter similar issues to those which have arisen in the field of Teaching English to Speakers of Other Languages (TESOL). Some of these include which variety(ies) of the language should be taught, the role of native and non-native speakers as teachers, issues of culture, identity and ownership of the language and their reflection in teaching practice, and if and how popular teaching methods such as Communicative Language Teaching (CLT) and Task Based Language Teaching (TBLT) can be used across all contexts. These are all additional lines of research which could be pursued as they apply to Chinese language education. Here it is interesting to note the emergence of the field of Teaching Chinese to Speakers of Other Languages (TCSOL).[1] The existence of Master degrees in TCSOL at many Chinese universities and the publication of academic journals in China and elsewhere show that this is a developing academic discipline. Of particular note is the journal *Global Chinese*, which commenced publication in 2015, and is specifically focused on studying the language, its teaching and learning on a global level. Some of the recent articles in this journal have dealt with these issues, including Fang and Duff's (2018) article on the use of Chinese popular culture in language teaching and its implications for learner identity, Zhang and Zhang's (2018) article on teacher identity among non-native speaker teachers of Chinese in higher education institutions in Denmark and Zhao's (2020) article on localising the Chinese language curriculum of an Australian primary school.

All of the above mentioned issues are well-established research topics in TESOL with a large body of literature on them (summaries and reviews of which can be found in Galloway & Rose, 2015; Jenkins, 2014; Kirkpatrick, 2007). As such, there is potential to draw insights and make comparisons, and for TESOL researchers and practitioners to share expertise and cooperate with colleagues working in Chinese language education.

Applied linguists and other scholars interested in language can make a valuable contribution to understanding "Chinese fever" through pursuing these lines of research and exploring their applications and implications.

NOTE

1. Academic research into the teaching and learning of Chinese as a second/additional language has of course existed for a long time. The point I am highlighting here is that the use of the name Teaching Chinese to Speakers of Other Languages (TCSOL) to label the academic study and practice of teaching Chinese as a second/additional language in parallel to Teaching English to Speakers of Other Languages (TESOL) is recent, and is a reflection of the growing global status of Chinese.

REFERENCES

Ammon, U. (2013). World languages: Trends and futures. In N. Coupland (Ed.), *The handbook of language and globalization* (pp. 101–122). Wiley-Blackwell.

Asia Education Foundation. (2010). *The current state of Chinese, Indonesian, Japanese and Korean language education in Australian schools: Four languages, four stories.* Education Services Australia. Retrieved 4 April, 2021, from https://www.asiaeducation.edu.au/docs/default-source/Research-reports/overarchingreport.pdf

Cheng, Y. (2021, January 13). 'China-watching' is a lucrative business. But whose language do the experts speak? *The Guardian.* Retrieved 4 March, 2021, from https://www.theguardian.com/commentisfree/2021/jan/13/understand-china-speak-chinese-english-language

Dörnyei, Z. (2007). *Research methods in applied linguistics: Quantitative, qualitative, and mixed methodologies.* Oxford University Press.

Duff, P. A. (2006). Beyond generalizability: Contextualization, complexity, and credibility in applied linguistics research. In M. Chalhoub-Deville, C. A. Chapelle, & P. Duff (Eds.), *Inference and generalizability in applied linguistics: Multiple perspectives* (pp. 65–95). John Benjamins Publishing Company.

Elder, C., Kim, H., & Knoch, U. (2012). Documenting the diversity of learner achievements in Asian languages using common measures. *Australian Review of Applied Linguistics, 35*(3), 251–270.

Fang, S., & Duff, P. (2018). Constructing identities and negotiating ideologies with Chinese popular culture in adult Mandarin learning. *Global Chinese, 4*(1), 37–61.

Galloway, N., & Rose, H. (2015). *Introducing global Englishes.* Routledge.

Huang, F. (2019, March 20). The actual worth of Chinese language proficiency. *SupChina.* Retrieved 2 March, 2021, from https://supchina.com/2019/03/20/the-actual-worth-of-chinese-language-proficiency/

Jenkins, J. (2014). *Global Englishes: A resource book for students* (3rd ed.). Routledge.

Kirkpatrick, A. (2007). *World Englishes: Implications for international communication and English language teaching.* Cambridge University Press.

Lo Bianco, J. (2012). Afterword: Tempted by targets, tempered by results. *Australian Review of Applied Linguistics, 35*(3), 359–361.

Lou, J. J. (2012). Chinatown in Washington, DC: The bilingual landscape. *World Englishes, 31*(1), 34–47.

Orton, J. (2008). *Chinese language education in Australian schools* (3rd ed.). The University of Melbourne. Retrieved 4 April, 2021, from https://www.asiaeducation.edu.au/docs/default-source/Research-reports/chinareport.pdf?sfvrsn=2

Orton, J. (2016). *Building Chinese language capacity in Australian.* Australia-China Relations Institute (ACRI). Retrieved 4 April, 2021, from https://www.australiachinarelations.org/sites/default/files/20032%20ACRI%20Jane%20Orton%20-%20Chinese%20Language%20Capacity_web_0.pdf

Singh, M., & Han, J. (2015). Making Chinese learnable: Strategies for the retention of language learners. In F. Dervin (Ed.), *Chinese educational migration and student-teacher mobilities* (pp. 166–190). Palgrave Macmillan.

Stebbins, R. A. (2001). *Exploratory research in the social sciences.* Sage.

Vaish, V. (2010). Introduction: Globalization of language and culture in Asia. In V. Vaish (Ed.), *Globalization of language and culture in Asia: The impact of globalization processes on language* (pp. 1–13). Continuum.

Wang, X., Chern, K. Y., Riget, P. N., & Shoniah, S. (2016). From monolingualism to multilingualism: The linguistic landscape in Kuala Lumpur's Chinatown. In W. Li (Ed.), *Multilingualism in the Chinese diaspora worldwide: Transnational connections and local social realities* (pp. 177–195). Routledge.

Zhang, C., & Zhang, Y. (2018). Language teacher identity construction: Insights from non-native Chinese-speaking teachers in a Danish higher educational context. *Global Chinese, 4*(2), 271–291.

Zhao, K. (2020). Localising Chinese language curriculum construction: A case study in an Australian primary school. *Global Chinese, 6*(2), 263–288.

Appendix 1: Questionnaire for Chinese Language Learners

This questionnaire is about your reasons for learning Chinese and your experiences learning Chinese.

You can answer Questions 1–8, 10–13, 15 and 16 by *circling* the option that applies to you. You can answer Question 9 by *circling* the option that applies to you and writing a *few sentences* or some *keywords*, and answer Questions 14 and 17 by writing a *few sentences* or some *keywords*.

The whole questionnaire should take you no longer than **10–15 minutes** to complete.

1. What is your age?
   18–24   25–34   35–40   Above 40

2. What is your gender?
   Male   Female

3. What is your native language?
   English   Other (please specify):

4. How long have you been learning Chinese?
   Less than 1 year 1–2 years 2–3 years 3–4 years More than 4 years

5. At what level of education did you start learning Chinese?
   Primary school Secondary school University Other (please specify):

6. What level of Chinese are you currently studying?
   First year Second year Third year Fourth year Other (please specify):

7. Where are you currently studying Chinese?
   Australia   China

8. How would you rate your current proficiency in Chinese?

   a. Speaking: Limited   Fair   Good   Very good   Excellent

   b. Listening: Limited   Fair   Good   Very good   Excellent

   c. Reading: Limited   Fair   Good   Very good   Excellent

   d. Writing: Limited   Fair   Good   Very good   Excellent

9. On a scale of 0–10 where 0 represents "*not important at all*" and
   10 represents "*extremely important*", how important were each of
   the following reasons in your decision to learn Chinese?

   a. Many governments and international organisations have policies
      which encourage the use of Chinese
      0   1   2   3   4   5   6   7   8   9   10
      Please explain why you chose this option. Please write a *few
      sentences* or some *keywords*.

      _____
      _____
      _____
      _____

   b. China is becoming more and more important in world affairs
      0   1   2   3   4   5   6   7   8   9   10
      Please explain why you chose this option. Please write a *few
      sentences* or some *keywords*.

      _____
      _____
      _____

c. China has a prestigious and popular traditional and contemporary culture and Chinese is a means to access this culture

0   1   2   3   4   5   6   7   8   9   10

Please explain why you chose this option. Please write a *few sentences* or some *keywords*.

_____

_____

_____

d. China's economy is developing rapidly and its economic power is high

0   1   2   3   4   5   6   7   8   9   10

Please explain why you chose this option. Please write a *few sentences* or some *key words*.

_____

_____

_____

e. Chinese is spoken by a large number of people and is learnt as a second or additional language by a large number of people around the world

0   1   2   3   4   5   6   7   8   9   10

Please explain why you chose this option. Please write a *few sentences* or some *keywords*.

_____

_____

_____

f. Chinese has a well-developed written script which can be used for all purposes

0   1   2   3   4   5   6   7   8   9   10

Please explain why you chose this option. Please write a *few sentences* or some *keywords*.

_____

_____

g. New developments and advances in the fields of science and technology are made in China and Chinese is a means to access information about such advances and developments
0   1   2   3   4   5   6   7   8   9   10
Please explain why you chose this option. Please write a *few sentences* or some *keywords*.

h. The quality of education and scholarly research in China are high and Chinese is a means to access education and research
0   1   2   3   4   5   6   7   8   9   10
Please explain why you chose this option. Please write a *few sentences* or some *keywords*.

10. How often do you watch Chinese movies?
Frequently   Sometimes   Seldom   Never

11. How often do you watch Chinese television programs?
Frequently   Sometimes   Seldom   Never

12. How often do you read Chinese novels?
Frequently   Sometimes   Seldom   Never

13. How often do you look at Chinese websites?
Frequently   Sometimes   Seldom   Never

14. Do you participate in any Chinese cultural activities, for example martial arts, cooking, calligraphy? Please list them.

_____
_____
_____
_____

15. How often do you participate in these Chinese cultural activities?
Frequently   Sometimes   Seldom   Never

16. What is the most difficult aspect of learning the Chinese language?
Tones
Pronunciation
Grammar
Characters/writing
Other (please specify): _____

17. Are there any features of the Chinese language you think make it an easy language to learn? Please write a *few sentences* or some *keywords*.

_____
_____
_____
_____

Would you be willing to participate in an *email interview* to further discuss various aspects of the questionnaire? If so, please write your email address here: _____

Thank you for your participation in this study.

Appendix 2: Email Interview Questions for Chinese Language Learners

1. Do you think the ability to speak Chinese will become more important in the future? Why/why not?
2. Do you think it is important for foreigners (i.e. people from non-Chinese backgrounds) to be able to speak Chinese? Why/why not?
3. Would you recommend learning Chinese to your friends and family? Why/why not?
4. What difficulties or challenges have you experienced in learning Chinese?
5. Do you think Chinese will replace English as the global language one day? Why/why not?

© The Editor(s) (if applicable) and The Author(s), under exclusive licence to Springer Nature Switzerland AG 2021
J. Gil, *The Rise of Chinese as a Global Language*,
https://doi.org/10.1007/978-3-030-76171-4

APPENDIX 3: CHINESE LANGUAGE LEARNER DEMOGRAPHIC DETAILS

Chinese Language Learner (CLL) Number	Age Range	Gender	Native Language	Length of Chinese Study	Level of Education Began Chinese Study	Level of Chinese Currently Studying	Country of Study	Self-rating of Current Proficiency in Chinese
CLL 1	18–24	Male	English	Less than 1 year	University	First year	Australia	S: Limited L: Limited R: Limited W: Limited
CLL 2	18–24	Male	Tagalog	Less than 1 year	University	First year	Australia	S: Limited L: Limited R: Limited W: Limited
CLL 3	18–24	Female	English	Less than 1 year	University	First year	Australia	S: Limited L: Limited R: Fair W: Fair
CLL 4	18–24	Female	English	Less than 1 year	University	First year	Australia	S: Fair L: Limited R: Fair W: Fair

(continued)

J. Gil, *The Rise of Chinese as a Global Language*, https://doi.org/10.1007/978-3-030-76171-4

(continued)

Chinese Language Learner (CLL) Number	Age Range	Gender	Native Language	Length of Chinese Study	Level of Education Began Chinese Study	Level of Chinese Currently Studying	Country of Study	Self-rating of Current Proficiency in Chinese
CLL 5	18–24	Female	English	Less than 1 year	University	First year	Australia	S: Fair L: Good R: Good W: Good
CLL 6	25–34	Female	English	Less than 1 year	Completed Bachelor degree	First year	Australia	S: Limited L: Limited R: Limited W: Limited
CLL 7	18–24	Female	English	Less than 1 year	University	First year	Australia	S: Limited L: Limited R: Fair W: Good
CLL 8	18–24	Male	English	1–2 years	Secondary school	Second year	Australia	S: Fair L: Good R: Good W: Limited
CLL 9	18–24	Female	English	1–2 years	University	Second year	Australia	S: Fair L: Fair R: Good W: Good
CLL 10	18–24	Male	English	Less than 1 year	University	First year	Australia	S: Limited L: Limited R: Limited W: Limited
CLL 11	18–24	Female	Malay	2–3 years	Secondary school	First year	Australia	S: Limited L: Limited R: Very good W: Very good
CLL 12	18–24	Female	Japanese	3–4 years *wrote "slow/basic" above selection*	Secondary school	First year	Australia	S: Good L: Very good R: Very good W: Good

(continued)

(continued)

Chinese Language Learner (CLL) Number	Age Range	Gender	Native Language	Length of Chinese Study	Level of Education Began Chinese Study	Level of Chinese Currently Studying	Country of Study	Self-rating of Current Proficiency in Chinese
CLL 13	18–24	Male	English	Less than 1 year	University	First year	Australia	S: Fair L: Fair R: Very good W: Good
CLL 14	18–24	Male	English	Less than 1 year	University	First year	Australia	S: Limited L: Limited R: Limited W: Limited
CLL 15	35–40	Female	English	Less than 1 year	University	First year	Australia	S: Good L: Fair R: Very good W: Good
CLL 16	18–24	Female	Vietnamese	Less than 1 year	University	First year	Australia	S: Fair L: Fair R: Fair W: Fair
CLL 17	Above 40	Male	English	2–3 years	University and Other: non-award after hours course at a university	Second year	Australia	S: Fair L: Fair R: Fair W: Fair
CLL 18	18–24	Male	English	2–3 years	University	Third year	Australia	S: Good L: Good R: Good W: Good
CLL 19	18–24	Male	English	Less than 1 year	University	First year	Australia	S: Limited L: Limited R: Limited W: Limited

(continued)

(continued)

Chinese Language Learner (CLL) Number	Age Range	Gender	Native Language	Length of Chinese Study	Level of Education Began Chinese Study	Level of Chinese Currently Studying	Country of Study	Self-rating of Current Proficiency in Chinese
CLL 20	18–24	Female	English	Less than 1 year	University	First year	Australia	S: Limited L: Limited R: Limited W: Limited
CLL 21	18–24	Female	English	Less than 1 year	University	First year	Australia	S: Limited L: Limited R: Limited W: Limited
CLL 22	18–24	Female	English	Less than 1 year	University	First year	Australia	S: Limited L: Limited R: Limited W: Limited
CLL 23	25–34	Female	Spanish	Less than 1 year	University	Other: not currently studying Chinese but did one semester of Chinese just prior to survey	Australia	S: Limited L: Limited R: Limited W: Limited
CLL 24	18–24	Male	English	Less than 1 year	University	First year	Australia	S: Fair L: Limited R: Fair W: Limited
CLL 25	18–24	Male	Finnish	Less than 1 year	University	First year	China	S: Limited L: Limited R: Limited W: Limited to Fair

(continued)

(continued)

Chinese Language Learner (CLL) Number	Age Range	Gender	Native Language	Length of Chinese Study	Level of Education Began Chinese Study	Level of Chinese Currently Studying	Country of Study	Self-rating of Current Proficiency in Chinese
CLL 26	18–24	Male	German	Less than 1 year	University	First year	China	S: Limited L: Limited R: Limited W: Limited
CLL 27	18–24	Female	Japanese	Less than 1 year	University	First year	China	S: Fair L: Fair R: Fair W: Good
CLL 28	25–34	Female	German	Less than 1 year	Other: language course after graduation	First year	China	S: Limited L: Limited R: Limited W: Limited
CLL 29	18–24	Female	English	Less than 1 year	University	First year	China	S: Limited L: Limited R: Limited W: Limited
CLL 30	18–24	Male	French	1–2 years	University	Third year	China	S: Good L: Fair R: Fair W: Fair
CLL 31	18–24	Male	English	Less than 1 year	University	First year	China	S: Excellent L: Excellent R: Limited W: Limited
CLL 32	18–24	Male	Finnish	1–2 years	University	Second year	China	S: Fair L: Fair R: Limited W: Fair

(continued)

(continued)

Chinese Language Learner (CLL) Number	Age Range	Gender	Native Language	Length of Chinese Study	Level of Education Began Chinese Study	Level of Chinese Currently Studying	Country of Study	Self-rating of Current Proficiency in Chinese
CLL 33	18–24	Male	Korean	Less than 1 year	University	First year	China	S: Fair L: Fair R: Fair W: Fair
CLL 34	18–24	Male	French	1–2 years	University	No response	China	S: Limited L: Fair R: Fair W: Fair
CLL 35	18–24	Male	Spanish	1–2 years	University	First year	China	S: Fair L: Limited R: Limited W: Limited
CLL 36	25–34	Female	English	Less than 1 year	University	First year	China	S: Limited L: Limited R: Fair W: Fair
CLL 37	25–34	Female	Korean	3–4 years	University	Fourth year	China	S: Good L: Good R: Very good W: Good
CLL 38	18–24	Female	Spanish	Less than 1 year	University	First year	China	S: Fair L: Good R: Good W: Good
CLL 39	18–24	Female	Malay	1–2 years	University	Second year	China	S: Good L: Very good R: Good W: Good
CLL 40	18–24	Male	Malay	Less than 1 year	University	Other: foundation	China	S: Limited L: Limited R: Limited W: Limited

(continued)

(continued)

Chinese Language Learner (CLL) Number	Age Range	Gender	Native Language	Length of Chinese Study	Level of Education Began Chinese Study	Level of Chinese Currently Studying	Country of Study	Self-rating of Current Proficiency in Chinese
CLL 41	18–24	Female	English	Less than 1 year	University	First year	China	S: Good L: Good R: Good W: Very good
CLL 42	18–24	Female	Russian	1–2 years	University	First year	China	S: Fair L: Fair R: Fair W: Fair
CLL 43	18–24	Male	Russian	2–3 years	University	Second year	China	S: Limited L: Limited R: Limited W: Limited
CLL 44	18–24	Female	English	2–3 years	University	Third year	China	S: Limited L: Limited R: Limited W: Limited
CLL 45	18–24	Female	Malay	1–2 years	University	First year	China	S: Fair L: Fair R: Fair W: Fair
CLL 46	18–24	Male	Malay	Less than 1 year	University	Other: foundation	China	S: Limited L: Limited R: Limited W: Limited
CLL 47	18–24	Female	Malay	Less than 1 year	University	Other: foundation	China	S: Limited L: Limited R: Limited W: Limited

(continued)

(continued)

Chinese Language Learner (CLL) Number	Age Range	Gender	Native Language	Length of Chinese Study	Level of Education Began Chinese Study	Level of Chinese Currently Studying	Country of Study	Self-rating of Current Proficiency in Chinese
CLL 48	25–34	Male	Portuguese	1–2 years	University	Second year	China	S: Limited L: Limited R: Limited W: Limited
CLL 49	18–24	Female	Malay	1–2 years	University	First year	China	S: Good L: Good R: Good W: Good
CLL 50	18–24	Female	Russian	Less than 1 year	University	First year	China	S: Fair L: Fair R: Fair W: Good
CLL 51	18–24	Female	Thai	1–2 years	Other: after graduation	First year	China	S: Fair L: Good R: Good W: Good
CLL 52	18–24	Female	Indonesian	1–2 years	Secondary school	First year	China	S: Fair L: Good R: Fair W: Fair
CLL 53	18–24	Male	English	1–2 years	University	Second year	China	S: Fair L: Fair R: Good W: Good
CLL 54	25–34	Female	Japanese	Less than 1 year	University	First year	China	S: Limited L: Limited R: Limited W: Limited
CLL 55	25–34	Female	Russian	2–3 years	Other: graduate	First year	China	S: Limited L: Limited R: Fair W: Fair
CLL 56	25–34	Male	Japanese	Less than 1 year	Other: work	First year	China	S: Fair L: Fair R: Good W: Good

(continued)

(continued)

Chinese Language Learner (CLL) Number	Age Range	Gender	Native Language	Length of Chinese Study	Level of Education Began Chinese Study	Level of Chinese Currently Studying	Country of Study	Self-rating of Current Proficiency in Chinese
CLL 57	25–34	Female	Spanish	1–2 years	Other: Master degree	First year	China	S: Limited L: Limited R: Good W: Fair
CLL 58	18–24	Female	English	1–2 years	University	Third year	China	S: Good L: Good R: Fair W: Limited
CLL 59	18–24	Female	Korean	1–2 years	University	Second year	China	S: Good L: Good R: Fair W: Fair
CLL 60	18–24	Female	Korean	1–2 years	University	Second year	China	S: Fair L: Good R: Good W: Very good
CLL 61	25–34	Male	Spanish	2–3 years	University	Second year	China	S: Fair L: Good R: Fair W: Limited
CLL 62	18–24	Female	Vietnamese	1–2 years	University	First year	China	S: Fair L: Fair R: Good W: Good
CLL 63	18–24	Male	English	Less than 1 year	University	First year	Australia	S: Limited L: Limited R: Limited W: Limited
CLL 64	18–24	Male	English	Less than 1 year	University	First year	Australia	S: Limited L: Limited R: Limited W: Limited

(continued)

(continued)

Chinese Language Learner (CLL) Number	Age Range	Gender	Native Language	Length of Chinese Study	Level of Education Began Chinese Study	Level of Chinese Currently Studying	Country of Study	Self-rating of Current Proficiency in Chinese
CLL 65	18–24	Female	English	Less than 1 year	University	First year	Australia	S: Limited L: Limited R: Limited W: Limited
CLL 66	17	Male	Cantonese	1–2 years	Primary school	First year	Australia	S: Excellent L: Excellent R: Very good W: Excellent
CLL 67	17	Female	English	Less than 1 year	University	First year	Australia	S: Limited L: Limited R: Limited W: Limited
CLL 68	25–34	Male	English	Less than 1 year	University	First year	Australia	S: Limited L: Limited R: Limited W: Limited
CLL 69	18–24	Male	Persian	1–2 years	Secondary school	First year	Australia	S: Limited L: Fair R: Fair W: Limited
CLL 70	Above 40	Male	English	Less than 1 year	University	First year	Australia	S: Limited L: Limited R: Limited W: Limited
CLL 71	18–24	Female	English	Less than 1 year	University	First year	Australia	S: Limited L: Fair R: Fair W: Limited

(continued)

(continued)

Chinese Language Learner (CLL) Number	Age Range	Gender	Native Language	Length of Chinese Study	Level of Education Began Chinese Study	Level of Chinese Currently Studying	Country of Study	Self-rating of Current Proficiency in Chinese
CLL 72	25–34	Female	English	Less than 1 year	Secondary school	First year	Australia	S: Fair L: Fair R: Limited W: Limited
CLL 73	25–34	Female	English	Less than 1 year	University	First year	Australia	S: Good L: Limited R: Good W: Good
CLL 74	18–24	Male	English	Less than 1 year	University	First year	Australia	S: Fair L: Good R: Good W: Fair
CLL 75	18–24	Female	English	Less than 1 year	University	First year	Australia	S: Fair L: Fair R: Fair W: Fair

Appendix 4: Interview Questions for Chinese Language Teachers (English & Chinese Versions)

1. In your opinion, which of these is the *most* important reason your students chose to learn Chinese? Please briefly explain why you chose this option.

a) Many governments and international organisations have policies which encourage the use of Chinese

b) China is becoming more and more important in world affairs

c) China has a prestigious and popular traditional and contemporary culture and Chinese is a means to access this culture

d) China's economy is developing rapidly and its economic power is high

e) Chinese is spoken by a large number of people and is learnt as a second or additional language by a large number of people around the world

f) Chinese has a well-developed written script which can be used for all purposes

g) New developments and advances in the fields of science and technology are made in China and Chinese is a means to access information about such advances and developments

h) The quality of education and scholarly research in China are high and Chinese is a means to access education and research

J. Gil, *The Rise of Chinese as a Global Language*, https://doi.org/10.1007/978-3-030-76171-4

2. In your opinion, which of these is the *least* important reason your students chose to learn Chinese? Please briefly explain why you chose this option.

a) Many governments and international organisations have policies which encourage the use of Chinese

b) China is becoming more and more important in world affairs

c) China has a prestigious and popular traditional and contemporary culture and Chinese is a means to access this culture

d) China's economy is developing rapidly and its economic power is high

e) Chinese is spoken by a large number of people and is learnt as a second or additional language by a large number of people around the world

f) Chinese has a well-developed written script which can be used for all purposes

g) New developments and advances in the fields of science and technology are made in China and Chinese is a means to access information about such advances and developments

h) The quality of education and scholarly research in China are high and Chinese is a means to access education and research

3. In your opinion, what is the most difficult aspect of learning the Chinese language for your students?

4. Are there any features of the Chinese language you think make it an easy language to learn?

5. Do you think the ability to speak Chinese will become more important in the future? Why/not?

6. Do you think Chinese will replace English as the global language one day? Why/why not?

Thank you for your participation in this study.

针对汉语教学人员的采访问题:

1. 您认为您的学生选择学习汉语的最重要原因是什么?请简述您选项的原因

   a) 很多政府与国际机构都有鼓励汉语应用的政策
   b) 中国的世界地位越来与重要
   c) 中国有着灿烂瞩目的传统与现代文化, 而汉语是领略此文化的重要手段
   d) 中国的经济发展迅速且其经济力量强大
   e) 汉语拥有庞大的使用人群, 且全球将汉语作为外语或第二外语学习的人数巨大。
   f) 汉语的书写体系发展完备且适用于各领域。
   g) 中国在科技领域取得飞速发展并在某系领域处于领先地位, 而汉语则是了解此信息的重要途径。
   h) 中国的教学和科研水平高, 汉语是获取中国教育与科研的重要途径

2. 您觉得, 以下哪一项是你学生选择学习汉语的最次要原因? 请简述您选项的原因

   a) 很多政府与国际机构都有鼓励汉语应用的政策
   b) 中国的世界地位越来与重要
   c) 中国有着灿烂瞩目的传统与现代文化, 而汉语是领略此文化的重要手段
   d) 中国的经济发展迅速且其经济力量强大
   e) 汉语拥有庞大的使用人群, 且全球将汉语作为外语或第二外语学习的人数巨大。
   f) 汉语的书写体系发展完备且适用于各领域。
   g) 中国在科技领域取得飞速发展并在某系领域处于领先地位, 而汉语则是了解此信息的重要途径。
   h) 中国的教学和科研水平高, 汉语是获取中国教育与科研的重要途径

3. 您觉得您的学生学习汉语过程中最大的困难时什么?
4. 你觉得汉语的哪些特点使汉语学习变得简单?
5. 您觉得能过说汉语会在将来变成一项重要技能吗? 为什么?
6. 你觉得有一天汉语会代替英语成为世界通用语言吗? 为什么?

衷心感谢您的参与

APPENDIX 5: INTERVIEW QUESTIONS FOR CHINESE SCHOLARS (ENGLISH & CHINESE VERSIONS)

1. In your opinion, which of these is the *most* important reason foreigners chose to learn Chinese? Please briefly explain why you chose this option.

   a) Many governments and international organisations have policies which encourage the use of Chinese

   b) China is becoming more and more important in world affairs

   c) China has a prestigious and popular traditional and contemporary culture and Chinese is a means to access this culture

   d) China's economy is developing rapidly and its economic power is high

   e) Chinese is spoken by a large number of people and is learnt as a second or additional language by a large number of people around the world

   f) Chinese has a well-developed written script which can be used for all purposes

   g) New developments and advances in the fields of science and technology are made in China and Chinese is a means to access information about such advances and developments

   h) The quality of education and scholarly research in China are high and Chinese is a means to access education and research

2. In your opinion, which of these is the *least* important reason foreigners chose to learn Chinese? Please briefly explain why you chose this option.

   a) Many governments and international organisations have policies which encourage the use of Chinese
   b) China is becoming more and more important in world affairs
   c) China has a prestigious and popular traditional and contemporary culture and Chinese is a means to access this culture
   d) China's economy is developing rapidly and its economic power is high
   e) Chinese is spoken by a large number of people and is learnt as a second or additional language by a large number of people around the world
   f) Chinese has a well-developed written script which can be used for all purposes
   g) New developments and advances in the fields of science and technology are made in China and Chinese is a means to access information about such advances and developments
   h) The quality of education and scholarly research in China are high and Chinese is a means to access education and research

3. In your opinion, what is the most difficult aspect of learning the Chinese language for foreigners?
4. Are there any features of the Chinese language you think make it an easy language to learn?
5. Do you think the ability to speak Chinese will become more important in the future? Why/not?
6. Do you think Chinese will replace English as the global language one day? Why/why not?

Thank you for your participation in this study.

<u>针对中国学者的采访问题</u>:

1. 您认为外国人选择学习汉语的最重要原因是什么？请简述您选项的原因

   a) 很多政府与国际机构都有鼓励汉语应用的政策
   b) 中国的世界地位越来与重要
   c) 中国有着灿烂瞩目的传统与现代文化，而汉语是领略此文化的重要手段
   d) 中国的经济发展迅速且其经济力量强大
   e) 汉语拥有庞大的使用人群，且全球将汉语作为外语或第二外语学习的人数巨大。
   f) 汉语的书写体系发展完备且适用于各领域。
   g) 中国在科技领域取得飞速发展并在某系领域处于领先地位，而汉语则是了解此信息的重要途径。
   h) 中国的教学和科研水平高，汉语是获取中国教育与科研的重要途径

2. 您觉得，以下哪一项是外国人选择学习汉语的最次要原因？请简述您选项的原因

   a) 很多政府与国际机构都有鼓励汉语应用的政策
   b) 中国的世界地位越来与重要
   c) 中国有着灿烂瞩目的传统与现代文化，而汉语是领略此文化的重要手段
   d) 中国的经济发展迅速且其经济力量强大
   e) 汉语拥有庞大的使用人群，且全球将汉语作为外语或第二外语学习的人数巨大。
   f) 汉语的书写体系发展完备且适用于各领域。
   g) 中国在科技领域取得飞速发展并在某系领域处于领先地位，而汉语则是了解此信息的重要途径。
   h) 中国的教学和科研水平高，汉语是获取中国教育与科研的重要途径

3. 您觉得外国人学习汉语过程中最大的困难时什么？
4. 你觉得汉语的哪些特点使汉语学习变得简单？
5. 您觉得能过说汉语会在将来变成一项重要技能吗？为什么？
6. 你觉得有一天汉语会代替英语成为世界通用语言吗？为什么？

衷心感谢您的参与

INDEX

© The Editor(s) (if applicable) and The Author(s), under exclusive   181
licence to Springer Nature Switzerland AG 2021
J. Gil, *The Rise of Chinese as a Global Language*,
https://doi.org/10.1007/978-3-030-76171-4